Thou Shalt Not Judge

Or

Unwanted Love

Or

The Most Disrespectful Book Ever Written

Dedication and Overview

To those who just want to be who they are. To hang out with those they want to hang out with, their friends; love who they love. To those who are constantly being corrected by those who claim they themselves are constantly being told what they are doing is wrong. To those who are silenced and ordered to fess up. To those who are ordered to think a certain way, and are exhausted and feel guilty about failing to just make themself into a different person. To those who are lectured, preached to, and altogether drowned in guilt. To those who are told they are unpredictable by those whom they cannot predict. To those who are manipulated and simply want to breathe. To those whom things have been read into so long that it is now become true; everything you ever thought was off limits and / or would never happen, has. To those who move away from everything, compulsory without any say. To those whose parents care about what they deem important. To those whose parents take any defence or even explanation and dish out a black and white demeaning declaration that it's an excuse. To those whose parents read my books at though they were The Screwtape Letters, thinking I'm on their side. To those who want to get away from their parents so bad they just want to kill themselves. Know that your pain is real. Know that your pain does matter. This one goes out to you. This one's for you.

Quotes

"*Of all tyrannies, a tyranny sincerely exercised for the good of its victims may be the most oppressive. It would be better to live under robber barons than under omnipotent moral busybodies. The robber baron's cruelty may sometimes sleep, his cupidity may at some point be satiated, but those who torment* us for our own good will torment us without end for they do so with the approval of their own conscience. " - Clive Staples Lewis

" If you Love something, set it free. If it comes back to you than it's yours; If not than it never truly was " - Hippie Proverb

" Judge not, lest you also be judged. For by what measure you judge; you yourself will also be judged " - Jesus

" Ok [name removed] I can only keep you safe if I wrap you up in bubble wrap and have you sit in a corner all day " - Anonymous

" Back in the day a child could run away from home and survive on their own. Nowadays those few that do manage to get away live horrific lives; and anyone that dares shelter them goes to prison. Nowadays all children are completely and 100% at the mercy of their parents; barring a few extremes. It truly proves the law of unintended consequences. " says W.X.Y.Z. Olaf. He also mentioned how a benevolent dictator; is still a dictator. Olaf has initiated an investigation into this case to see how the parents may be criminally responsible, what all for. Also he is attempting to have an investigation into the military school / boot camp initiated. The brother has not been accused of any crime in these proceedings " – Paragraph removed from *Last Grafts*

" But he struck my brother!...Whatever Count Olaf has done...he has acted in loco parentis, and there's nothing I can do about it. Your money will be well protected by myself and by the bank, but Count Olaf's parenting techniques are his own business. Now, I hate to usher you out posthaste, but I have very much work to do " – Chapter five, The Bad Beginning, A Series of Unfortunate Events by Lemony Snicket

" No Buts! " – every dictator ever

" Kids being bullied need to just learn to toughen up " – Anonymous teacher

Fictionalized Ideological horror

Factious Plot; real concerns

Inspired By Actual Events

Chapter One

Emergency Services

"Inspectors just finished up; normally they wouldn't even bother to see about foul play. But this, I've never even heard of this. But with no evidence indicating homicide, guess it really was…" said the paramedic.

"Yeah, just finished giving my statement, I heard what I was saying and I couldn't believe me; and I knew it to be true. I'd seen it first-hand!" said the homeowner.

"I know what you mean, I-I, just, How-how can things seen so bad; be so bad, that this, this would seem the only way out, preferable in the slightest?! I just can't get my head around it-" said the paramedic.

"Hey, just letting you know. Coroner's removed the bodies; we're going to impound the car," said a policeman.

"Whatever, not even my car. Even if it was I wouldn't want it now!" said the homeowner.

"Yeah, can't exactly be good for Kelly Blue-" he quickly shut himself up. Judging from the looks he was getting; nothing could have been in worse taste.

"You find any suicide notes?" said the homeowner.

"More than you can shake a stick at," said the paramedic.

"What did they say?" said the homeowner.

He simply shook his head.

"I-I don't understand?" said the homeowner.

"Sir, you need to make a statement, so we can file a breaking and entering report for your insurance," said a policewoman.

"Breaking and entering?" said the homeowner and the paramedic.

"Well, technically they did break in-" she said.

"No, I let the place while I went on a long trip in Europe to some guy on air B&E, I mean B&B. Besides, no damage was done and nothing was lost that could be calculated in dollars," said the homeowner.

"Actually I'm afraid we found a spot where coolant boiled over and dried onto the floor of your-" she realized some chemical stain was the last thing anyone would ever be concerning themselves with.

"You knew the victims, right?" she said.

"Hardly, didn't recognize a one. And before you point out that I identified the driver, or that is the man in the driver's seat. I had to look that up. Even then I wasn't, still am not certain. Just a resemblance," said the homeowner.

"Think it might not actually be him?" he said.

"Not a snowball's chance in a non-Dantean hell." said the homeowner. Everyone paused and looked puzzled. "Centuries old book; in it the center of hell was frozen. Mandatory reading; you didn't miss much" said the homeowner.

"I know I didn't enjoy Walden, sense never read a memoir. Wait, how are you so sure?" said the paramedic.

"Simple, had his phone number, called in. Heard a ringtone from in the car. Which I suppose technically could have simply been put there " said the homeowner, "Say, are you sure it's safe to be in here, I mean I've heard that the house will also eventually fill up with-"

"Yeah, car had been running so long it completely died; sense enough time has passed for the ac to have replaced the air supply several times over." said the paramedic, "My superior told me so."

"Wait, why didn't the battery die?" said the policewoman.

"Was running a long time. Probably ran out of gas, but the battery was juiced up," said the paramedic, "I saw it plugged in."

"You know, when I let the house; I knew the homeowners' association didn't allow you to let your house, especially briefly to tourists. At that point in time I just didn't care. And now. After what's happened. I still don't care!" he said.

"Well, I imagine the homeowners' accusation will now have found out." said the paramedic.

"The homeowners' accusation can go screw itself!" said the homeowner "For the record, I normally don't talk that way."

"In the middle of this; F bombs would be justified," said the paramedic, "How you gunu live here after this?"

"Oh I won't! Gunu hafta sell this place," said the homeowner.

"Well, you'll no doubt have to disclose it as a haunted house," said the paramedic.

"Funny you should mention a haunted house. One was at least done up as a goth." said the homeowner.

"I saw," said the paramedic, who paused and said "I'm Not Even Sure They Were All Even Teenagers!"

"It's just, just, just, Why?! What?! I-I mean I-I" said the homeowner. By this point they were both about to completely loose it.

"You want answers," said the paramedic.

"Yeah, yeah, I want answer," said the homeowner.

"Me too, I want answers," said the paramedic.

"Then let's get some answers" said the homeowner.

"Yeah, yeah let's get some answers. said the paramedic.

Chapter Two

Rebel

"No cuts, no butts, no paper cuts" It was said almost like a sick nursery rhyme. Or at least it sounded that way.

"But Dad-" he said.

"I Said No Buts Zion!" that was in an extremely authoritative voice. A voice you would never dream of questioning.

"Do you realize what you're doing to us?!" said the mother, sounding like she was going to cry.

"You're such a disgrace! You get into so much trouble that we have to have you sent off. Then you have the gaul to get into so much trouble that they actually give up on you?!!?"

"We're trying to do right by you, and you don't even seem to care,"

"Yes, we're making sacrifices so you can be straightened out and you just spit it back in our face"

"Your mother's right son, you don't care about us you just want what you want, when you want it, how you want it"

"Exactly, we're putting our foot down."

"But Dad-"

"NO BUTS SON AND DO NOT INTERUPT. We've found a place that will take you. Maybe they can straighten you out." By then he had bulging veins in his neck.

"And don't even think of an escape attempt. We'll be watching you around the clock. We've already put bells so we can hear if you try an escape. And don't try enlisting your sister. We're keeping her away from you. After what you've done, no telling what you'd do to her. Now Zion I will escort you to your room.

Rebel woke up drenched in a cold sweat. He loathed reliving that fight. He was so silenced. So powerless.

"Stupid flashback dream" he said aloud.

He had had many fights like that, in fact they usually went on for hours, until he apologized and claimed to fully agree with them. It was a lie. But he had to submit. It was required. Backtalk and disrespect was taboo.

BELCH! Rebel put the carton back in the refrigerator.

That was a long time ago. When he hit 18 he left that camp and went into a homeless shelter. His family absolutely hated him for it. Well, almost all of his family. He hadn't seen his little sister for years; and when he changed his name, he was permanently banished. He missed her. If he had had any money we would have hired a private investigator to see to it that she was ok. He had called Child Protective Services in the past. But of no avail. He had also tried to have the transformation camp investigated. But everyone he talked to just couldn't see past a juvenile record, they just weren't able. He decided to flip on the idiot box.

"With IKEA you can completely transform your living space on a budg-"

"Gahh!" he groaned. Sometimes things would just catapult him backwards. The last and most heinous facility. They used words like transformation and Summer Camp for at risk youths. Sound's innocent enough; but when you had the implications. It was bone chilling. The Nazis were obsessed with purity, being purely German. And while that may sound like a demining anti-Semitic and anti-Romany comment. What you should know is that years before all this began to hit the fan he once went camping in the California foothills; all thought-out which he had to keep reminding himself he was not in Colorado. In the throes of this he had to keep reminding himself he was not in the Hanoi Hilton. All the more reason he appreciated veterans. It wasn't like he was forced into a Capitulate position till he submitted, Rather they just kept forcing their propaganda into his mind, forcing it onto him. It was horrible. Even if they were right! He had to just "Carry the Truth." He had to assist and carry on the propaganda. It was treated almost as if they were treating the ill. They were twisting and carving his psyci into a perpetuation and manifestation of their idea of an ideal citizen. The whole time he was in shock; which actually wasn't even a bad thing. A cosmic mercy he supposed; a little bit like why Harper Lee thought people passed out in pain. Don't get it wrong. He had been to military schools and boot camps before. They were bad, and they also left him with memories he wanted so badly to escape. They too bowed down and prostrated before the altar of order. And God were they ever orderly. There they wanted what they wanted, how they wanted, where they wanted, when they wanted, and with what they wanted. And may God have had mercy on your soul if you ever put one toe out of line, or you showed anything but the utmost and absolute proper respect. But if you think purgatory is bad; wait till you see the Lake of Fire. All along he thought he was already experiencing hell on earth. All along he thought they were blowing smoke. Till they weren't. Contrary to how they saw it. He almost always went along with they said. And they were nice when he made a decision they agreed with; assuming it can be called a decision when they would allow him to decide for himself when he made the correct decision. But when he had the audacity to make a decision that they disagreed with…

"You will apologize for what you have done! I will not allow you to go on- JESUS!" The girl screamed.

She had handcuffed herself to a post. Things would be out of line and they would not have absolute, final, and complete authority. They had to act quick. To protect and re-institute order they grabbed an axe and chopped her hand clean off. She was quickly removed.

"Rugh!" groaned Rebel as he shook away the flashback. He had seen that girl afterward. But never again with her hand. He had always wanted to talk to her; but he never got the chance. Like prisoners at Guantanamo or suspects separate for god forbid they have any opportunity to say a few subversive words or get their story straight. In that moment it hit him fully. Not matter what, there is no horror so great it truly cannot get worse and there really and truly is nothing they would not to institute order, respect, and all the other militaristic ideals they strived not for themselves, no they were perfectly the machines described by Thoreau[1]. But

---

[1] It had "Disobedience" it the title. How could Rebel not read it?

rather strived onto others. Absolutely nothing. It was the only time he saw a full-fledged show of barbarity. But it wasn't even close to the only horror or barbaric act. Just the single greatest barbaric act. They instead used means more subtle, never again, or before, as open and violent.

Flush! Rebel didn't wash up afterward. Walking out of the head he reached for the light.

Filp flip

"Great! Burnt out, well at least this time I've the money to replace you!" He glanced at the clock "Let's see what time it is, meh, either way an't getting anymore sleep till about time to wake up anyway. *Maybe I'll run down and get a new one. Only a couple of-"* Rebel realized what he said. Many women have said "You can take the bachelor out of the bachelor pad, but you can't take the bachelor pad out of the bachelor" similar rule of thumb Rebel realized was at play. They had tried so hard to force him into being a perfect southern gentleman. His deepest true self had changed. Many times people talk about feeling as though a part of them had changed. But what had happened was not like a part of him had died or even been murdered. No rather it was more like simply a fate worse than death. Through it all Rebel had felt like he was holding onto something, something intangible, about to lose his grip. Much like trying to stay awake with a chloroform rag over face. In much the same way he all along had felt It seeping in, draining away his personal liberty and right of freedom within his thought processes. Once he read a Parade article from a P.O.W. J.M. Stockdale. He described having all liberty robbed of him. Even that which must be as least somewhat voluntary was coerced out of him. He wasn't able to finish it. Rebel knew that any comparison with that to anything would only ever be seen as either blowing things out of proportion or to take away from one of the great horrors of history. Possibly both. Though all that had happened he could never have imagined what it would have been like to be there; and he was grateful for that fact. In fact the hand-horror was the only act of gross violence that he ever saw firsthand[2]. There were those that disappeared. Though Rebel wondered, they could have been able to leave, or maybe, just maybe they escaped. You know what they say "It's all in your head"

---

[2] For once in the history of the human race there really and truly, no pun intended.

Another flashback hit Rebel. This time he was in fist fight with his friend Matthew. It was an all-out brawl. They enacted the boot-camp idea of punishing the group if one steps out of line. Sure if they went against a commander that was worse than burning down an orphanage. But if they went against each other. Well, divide and conquer. They would just bang each outer back into line. He didn't ever remember who or what it was. Just another brawl. Just another "Anything so that we can recreate you" Because we have a clue and you don't. Rebel tried to distract himself from that flashback

Rebel was in a place that no descent human could ever justify exerting. No one belonged there. But if anyone didn't belong it probably had been Matthew. He had been carted off there after what he called "A very successful rebellion at a Pray the Gay away camp" Sure there may have been some bragging. But Matthew was the only one Rebel ever made contact with afterwards. Even at that, only a few E-mails. They had slept together in the past; Rebel wasn't gay. And that wasn't why. Just anything to escape their horrible reality. Anything. As for after he got out. Rebel just couldn't go back. And as it was. It could still surprise him what send him back. He knew that the wrong sentence from someone could remind him all too well of some horrible terror. Something he might not be able to shove back to subconsous.

He had another flashback. This time they were out working. Grueling labor. The way they were treated, it went beyond robbing them of human dignity. It robbed them of mammalian dignity, there's just no other way to describe it. Rebel remembered how they should have been hospitalized for exhaustion. But that was about as likely as a politician keeping their campaign promises. Nevertheless, despite being worked to the bone, Rebel, then Zion, he could just look over and see his friend Jose. When they met he tried to lighten the mood my saying "That's a really unfortunate name. Because whenever you ask for something; people will simply reply 'no way Jose'" He had heard it before. And it became quickly apparent that it despite all that was happening. Jose had it even worse. His beginning was more innocent. He accidently broke something. And his domineering stepfather stuck by "Sorry's not going to fix this!" And absolutely made him earn the money to fix it. Well about the only way he could get money at his age where he lived was selling drugs. He got desperate, it all went sideways. By the time he (Jose) found himself detained there he was in the throes of withdrawal. Yet despite the agonizing aches, he was treated no different. He took to look out for Jose while he was there; but wasn't much he could do. This was no recovery program; no more than starvation was a diet. And starvation, not as in skipping meals. But rather as in being simply locked in a crate and forgotten. He did what he could for Jose, but that was not much. Usually when he tried to help someone out it backfired on not just them, but him, and others also.

By this time Rebel had decided to stay in for the night. It wasn't a safe area, and now that he was no longer working the graveyard shift there was no reason for him to go out in that danger. Another flashback hit him. This time he was discovering a trader. He saw the Cheeto yellow on his fingers clear as he relieved that moment. Only time they ever prevented a fight. He knew what had happened. After a moment Rebel was able to shake himself out of that flashback. He had to go sit down. It reminded him of an article he had read about holocaust snitches; course they called it something else. And obviously this was not a concentration camp. But the basic principle, the scamatics, inner workings are essentially the same. A bona-fide and in and of itself legitimate authority figure is incarcerating people some place for some reason. And to fully control the place and put down what-ever comes up, basically be all knowing. They solicit traders. Who themselves get better treatment, parole, early release, the candy confiscated from school detention. Basically it's the same ultimate structure.

"*Maybe I'll call and see if I can order a pizza from Pizzaiolo, no, no, it's too expensive. And besides, I highly doubt I could get them, to deliver a Pizza, to me, here, way across the East Bay, at this hour. And besides I'm already fat enough,*" Thought Rebel. And it's true, he had gained a lot of weight after getting out. Also he had only been able to get minimum wage-part time work.

buzz buzz

Rebel went to check his phone. Sure he had the cheapest lawyer money could buy; but he did work late, err, worked odd hours. Rebel gasped. Not a true gasp of surprise, rather the gasp of someone having heard that a dying relative has died. He had tried to sue his parents, the military schools, even child protective services. They all fell through. This was his last hope of any justice. He had even picked out a locked memory care ward in the slums of New York. Would claim to be moving there; if necessary he would. When he was there he saw mold on the walls, rodent droppings, and smelled oatmeal for dinner, among other odors. Also was pretty cheap too. He would have them experience what he went through! But he got this message. His parents had easily had it resolved. *Easily* Now any hope of any remote shred of justice would be gone. Was gone. Excepting the inevitability that is death. His parents were fat, last he heard high cholesterol. Probably would be quick, just a heart attack.

"Don't even get to say goodbye to my sister" he said aloud.

Chapter Three
Ash

"Happy birthday dear Ashley" sang everyone.

"Ouch!" said Kam.

"KIM! Don't interrupt. I should not have to correc-" said Marquesa.

"It's ok Mom," said Ash.

Kim felt her leg, and then looked at her fingers, blood. Not dangerous, but enough to stain. "Oy Vey" she said.

"You ok there?" whispered Kam's twin.

"Stop whispering, use' two. Now let's start again," said Marquesa.

"It-It's ok Mom-" said Ash.

"No it's not, she-" said Marquesa.

"No-no I-I just want cake," said Ash, mostly lying.

"Oh, ok. Let's cut the cake!" said Marquesa.

"You ok there?" said one relative.

"Don't" said the father, the adults' scornful glances kept her from coming over. The teens were too afraid to say anything.

"Sis, We can't make a fuss over every little everything. Or else we'll just baby them. You have to let them work it out on their own," said Marquesa.

Later

"So, guess you're now a teenager" said Igneous.

"Yeah, kill joy was this one thing with my sister-" said Ash.

"NO TALKING" they shouted.

"I loathe this school," whispered Ash.

From here on the conversation had to be done in secret

"By all rights it isn't a school, it's not about teaching lessons, just 'learning a lesson'" communicated Igneous.

"And nothing in the world is worth more than that lesson, including the educational lessons taught at the original schools," she communicated.

"How you holding up?" he asked.

"As well as could expected Ig," she communicated.

"About that thing at your party?" he asked.

"Oh, that was a 5 minute kill joy, we all just shrank back and gave in, and soon it was ok again, know what I mean?" she communicated.

"Ash, where are we?" he replied.

"Good point, but that was so commonplace a thing, fluke I even remember it. Happens all the time. Wish you could have been there" she communicated.

"You say that as if it were a good thing," he communicated.

"Well, I would like for you to have been able to be there," she communicated.

"No not that, that thing about commonplace," he communicated.

"Oh that, yeah, well, nothing could be done about it, so, as the French would say. "C'est le vie"[3]," she communicated.

"Well that sure makes it sound hopeless," he replied.

"Don't make it sound so dark. I'm not in military/boot camp school, so can't complain," she communicated.

"I wouldn't be so sure, as you may remember, there was a building, I forget where, somewhere in this city. When the fire safety system broke and filled it overflowing and to the street with foam. Did they have grounds for complaining, just because it didn't burn down?" he replied.

After a pause she replied "That's an interesting way of looking at things, but. I think this is one of those things that, you don't really want hope because if you think it may get better, then you will begin to believe that they either are better, or at least start expecting them to be better. And it just makes it all the more crushing, especially when in this case your reaction just makes them all the worse. And, and the worst part is, you'd just have to be in my head, I mean It's not the worst thing in the world, but. I-I could never hope to fully describe it. I'm sure it's just common teenage stuff. And as such it will always be chalked up by the world," she by this time had begun to have trouble being discreet.

Seeing the urgency of changing the subject, he communicated "About the party, how was it?"

---

[3] Translates-that is life

"Oh it was fun, Like I said, I wish you could have been there."

"Maybe next time I can, We've had this thing going on long enough. And now you really are a teenager. Maybe you could talk to them, or would that just, you know," he communicated.

"Oh it's not that bad, large reason I've been so quiet. It's like this. Oddly enough Mom decided to see one of the Twilight Saga movies when it was on. And Grandma, this is before she had passed. She was staying with us at the time, you know?" communicated Ash.

"I know," communicated Igneous.

"Well, Mom found it hard to live with her, guess what goes around comes around. Which just so happens to be an expression Grandma taught me. But Mom was this time really embroiled by when Her mother simply got up and left when it was playing. It's all like that," she communicated.

"Little subtle indicators," replied Igneous.

"Well, it's not really any one thing, no one thing is, and doubtful could ever be, that terrible. Rather, it's a cumative effect. But, if it is any one thing. It's that," communicated Ash.

"You think, maybe 50% is from that?" asked Igneous.

"Well, frankly your guess is as good as mine. But another issue is feeling forced to say something, pretend to like something, stay in something. That's been going on all my life. Course I imagine my brother is going through it worse," she replied.

"That how you ended up in brownies?" asked Igneous.

"Well, what New York girl is going to want to be a scout?" replied Ash.

"Never realized," he communicated.

Ash shrugged and replied "Had it not been for the move, probably would have been dragged all the way up to gold star," she communicated.

Igneous asked "Would you still move back to the Big Apple if given the choice?"

"I'd have to think on that. I've begun to set down roots. I-I probably would say yes if it was right this red hot second, or never. However on the other hand when things are now or never that alone tends to make me say never, but by this point I'm probably rambling," replied Ash.

"Well, I know in the past I could have never have bared to be uprooted like a non-sentient plant, and transplanted in a new pot away from all my friends and everything I know and love by some 'maturer than thou' gardener," he communicated.

"You already have," she realized.

"And like you, I too have found and made new connections in this horrible reality," he said.

"You're right. I am now a teenager. Old enough to join Facebook, course then I'd be cyber bullied by my parents and powerless to do anything but just submit and surrender and give up-" she communicated.

"Spiraling, but, where were you intending to go? With what you were communicating?" communicated Igneous.

"I think I'm old enough to come forward. But let's all pretend that we're just starting out," communicated Ash.

"Good Idea, I'll have to let Echo know first. We'll need out story straight," he communicated.

"And you're sure no one else knows?" asked Ash.

No reply came, the overseers were getting close to determining where the communication was coming from.

LATER

It took Ash 5 days to work up the nerve to ask her parents for a date night out.

"So, your first date?" he said.

"Well, yes dad," she said.

"So where you headed?" he said.

"Salumeria" she said.

"When you going out, that is what night?" he asked.

"Whatever night Kat is free to drive me, I suppose," she replied.

"Oh no, she's grounded, I'll take you," he said.

"*Wait, what?*" she thought "So, you want to drive me?"

"Oh yeah, we'll all have a good time," he replied.

"*Oh no*"

"Course, I'll have to meet him first, make sure my little girl's not falling in with the wrong crowd," he said.

"*Lord, I hope he's related to a Marine that's got time to tag along, or maybe a S.E.A.L.*"

And so went the evening. Igneous' wallet was inspected, he was watched lake a hawk. Ash regretted having ever gone out with him because it was just such a terrible experience. He was overbearing and intimidating. If anyone had been paying attention, then he might have been arrested for how he was acting. And as insult to injury, they were demeaned by being forced to pretend to be under twelve to they could order off the kids menu; he saved $4.84. Call it compensating errors; but when he heard how they met; he clearly wanted to get up and leave right then.

Later:

"Ashley I don't want you going out with that boy again," he said.

"Whatever *Just as well; in fact I'm happy. Gives me an out to prevent this horrible night from happening again*," said / thought Ash.

"Ahem!" he said.

Painfully, she said "Yes sir," it always hurt her to be forced to suck-up. *"Not enough to banish my boyfriend. Have to have the* Proper dignified respect *as well"* she thought mocking.

You know, it hurts me every time I hear you being impolite.

"It's 2*** you should not be embarrassed. If you're by my alleged rudeness; then maybe I get to be embarrassed by being seen with such a curmudgeon in public. My God! I should not have to explain this to a new Yorker!!" thought Ash.

Later the next school day at school.

"Guess that didn't go to well," communicated Igneous.

"If by not too well you mean, I'd rather switch to chasing other girls, then yes. That didn't go too well," replied Ash.

"That guy scares me," said Igneous.

"I told you to bring a big scary relative," communicated Ash.

"My grandparents met at Woodstock. The longest ponytail in my family is on a man, and so's the second. Who, that even could be intimidating or masculine has a ponytail?" he replied.

"Si Robertson," communicated Ash, seeing his baffled look she said "Not worth explaining."

"Well, maybe my dad could come along, give your dad a couple of 'Hey man's and have a similar effect," Joked Igneous.

"Fat chance, You probably realized he simply didn't want me to go out wit-" replied Ash.

"I knew that before I ever laid eyes on him," communicated Igneous.

"No, no. There was a point when it was clear and he was hinting that he just wanted to get up and leave," replied Ash.

"Like the start," replied Igneous.

"Good one-" Ash stopped herself, realizing that he wasn't joking. "There was a clear point where he all but asked if it would be ok if we left."

"He was having such a fit all night, I never knew the difference. Like one of those obnoxious stories Bubbie and Zada tell about when they were young." seeing her puzzled look, he added in "It's what I call my grandparents."

"What about if you simply pulled a Nancy Reagan and just said no?" communicated Igneous.

"Didn't go over too well when they didn't want me to go hang out with Mom's sisters," replied Ash.

"So now they're going after their own?!" he replied.

"Yeah pretty much. Ended up having to lie and say I agree and simply want what they wanted me to want. Sound's crazy, but true," communicated Ash.

"More a tongue twister, like how you ended up a brownie. And what was their bugaboo in the first place?" replied Igneous.

"First of all, like I said, what New York girl wants to be a scout? Second, they didn't go to Mass, or help with older relatives care, basically their relationship was poor and I was being dragged into it," communicated Ash.

"Jealous?" asked Igneous.

"Actually, I think it was simply a case of believing they are older therefore simply must know what's best, and trying to keep me an immaculate little bubble. And being in the big apple that was absolutely hopeless and made them overbearing," replied Ash.

"Must be pretty hypocritical, trying to keep you in purityland, while they won't give up their city life," communicated Igneous.

"THANK HEAVENS! Furthermore It's probably also largely career related; or at least partially career related," communicated Ash.

The conversation recessed for a while, then Ash blurted out, such that she was almost heard "How can he treat me this way!"

They pretended to be not paying any attention to each other for a while soasto wait for the heat to cool off. After a lengthy/significant pause, Igneous showed he hadn't quite caught that.

"How can he be so awful to me if he loves me? I mean does he-" answered Ash.

"As crazy as this may sound. I have come to the enlightenment that matters such as these-" communicated Igneous.

"You need to stop pontificating Mr. Dali Lama. And coming from a Catholic, that's really saying something," communicated Ash.

"Yes, yes. Well, I think it's because he loves you. He's trying to protect you-" communicated Igneous.

"But What He's Doing Is Horrible!" she communicated.

"Precisely, you see if he was bad he could, at least possibly, have a pang of guilt, or at least find something else to do. 'But those who torment us for our own good do so unrelentingly for they do so with the approval of their conscience' In fact the very mechanism, that is the conscience, which would at least help to restrain them, exempting psychopaths, pushes them forward. Because they think what they are doing is right they are kept doing it by guilt, and concern. And on they continue in their attempts to make the world a better place as best they know how. 'While they may be more likely to go to heaven, such people can sure make a real hell of earth'," communicated Igneous.

"Are you quoting someone? Because it sure sounds like a quote," communicated Ash.

"Probably, not sure who," replied Igneous.

"Well, if whoever that is, is right, then he must be quaking in utter terror," she communicated.

"Yeah, in his mature mind I'm sure he simply sees himself as protecting his baby from a juvenile- oh, you said that he didn't know how we," he communicated.

"He's just a real, true blue dad. You know he's dragged Crow out into the woods," she said.

"I thought that that was an excuse to get him away from-" he communicated.

"Just the timing was. But the weird part is, last night he seemed to, in spite of everything. He seemed to have a good time," she communicated.

"Far out, I'd have to guess. He was happy he had satisfied his great fear-" he communicated.

"Great fear of what? He-He's just quaking in absolute and utter terror that I might possibly have sex. That's it! Nothing more than an awesome and mighty terror-" she communicated.

"Maybe not even that much. You know as well as anyone else at Salumeria I could no more have kissed you than the man in the moon," he communicated.

So ended the conversation; Lunch period was over and that was the only time they were able to get together. And so it drifted back to day to day. Ash was now a teenage girl. But essentially she had passed a mile marker. Real changes in her life would come more gradually. She and her secret boyfriend grew closer and closer together; close enough she wouldn't leave him.

Sometime later:

"Ashley would you come in here," said Marquesa.

"Hi Mom," said Ash.

"I heard about what happened at school today," said her father.

"You did?" said Ash, "*Here we go.*"

"Yes, first day out and you get yourself back in!" said her father.

"*Well had to make sure I didn't get off with an in school suspension. Being shoved in a corner with busywork wouldn't do me any good,*" thought Ash.

"Do you have any idea what you're putting us through?!?! And on to of other things that are going on; things that you don't even know about," bemoaned Marquesa.

"*Really, of all the things you could say to me; you have to dish out guilt!?!? Your personal pity party,*" thought Ash.

"We're talking to out lawyer; hopefully you won't have to go before the court-" said her father.

"Say what now," said Ash.

"Yeah, he says it's your first time, so you won't be in too much trouble. But the school says you're a threat to safety. They'll have to expel you for the rest of the semester," said Marquesa. The way she said it, she may as well have said how much a disappointment Ash was.

"What!?!? That Schoolyard clesha? I'm not a-" said Ash.

"No Excuses! You're grounded until you get back in school," said her father.

"You attacked the principal. Hopefully we can get the sexual aspect pled out," bemoaned Marquesa.

"Why don't yo-" said Ash, completely cut off. Silenced.

"Go to your room," said her father, pontificating against her.

"But-" said Ash.

"Now Young Lady," he commanded, in a voice that you just don't question.

In that moment Ash became acutely aware she was powerless to her parents; beholden and dependent absolutely and complete.

"Why don't you sue? That schoolyard clesha; the way their bringing down the gavel. Hypocrisy! And I'm maybe a threat to the faculty, but being those in charge that, well. They're the ones that it matters if they get-" thought Ash.

Then Ash overheard something on her way out. Something she wasn't supposed to hear; but she did.

"You think that was enough?" said her dad.

"Yeah, good job bad cop-" said Marquesa.

Then she heard the giggling. It hit her like a ton of bricks. So much emotional distress she did good to make it back to her room at all. Where she collapsed and thrashed limbs angrily for no particular purpose like a ruminator[4].

"There's no such thing as love,"

Fortunately Ash's siblings were able to bail her out of being separated from her boyfriend. She had already had contact information for Igneous, and would borrow her Sib's mobile devices; which proved that Skyping in a closet, or wherever she could find was actually better than then communicating over a table, more lip-reading than actual speech, to hide it. She had feared that going back would serve as a re-boot. Things would be different. And she would live out the end of 1984 where they passed each other; and didn't even acknowledge each other. And despite as taboo as their love was it would prove to be helpful in a way the authority figures could never have been. As follows.

"I love you, you know that. Don't you?" said Igneous.

"There is no such thing as love," Ash blurted, feeling unusually blunt.

---

[4] From the psychological term rumination. Meaning something is really bothering you, such as news of horrible current events, so much so that it goes beyond merely obsessing over it.

"Say what? Ash, what was that you were trying to say?" he said.

"Igneous, there is no such thing as love. Parents just want submission, children just want privileges and stuff, lovers just want sex. Let's just stop kidding ourselves," said Ash.

"Who did what to you?" said Igneous.

"I simply realized, figured it out," said Ash.

"Figured it out, then why does God love us; or do you still believe in a higher power?" said Igneous.

"I've heard the science. I can't deny God to exist, or at the very least some higher power. But, I guess the same reason as any other parent," she said.

"You still believe what you heard about what love is-" he said.

"Patient, kind, etc… No-" she said.

"No, just in fiction. Could exist in a made up story, right?" he said.

"Yeah, at least that makes sense," she said.

"Well, why have your siblings lent you teck so we can stay together like this?" he said.

After a pause Ash finally replied, "Well, I guess they were hoping for something in return?" She really didn't have an answer.

"I was about to cut in and guess for your sake rebellion for the sake of rebellion. But never mind that. Ash, what if I convinced you that love did exist?" he said.

"Well, I suppose I would go back to the way I had been thinking. But good luck with that," she replied.

"Ash, why did you give that principal a wedgy so that you could go back to that horrible jail school?" he asked.

Somewhat dumbstruck she said "Well, I-I guess I-I like spending time with you-I-I-"

"Like being with me more than you hate the jail school, and that's not even accounting for the risk you might not be able to see me on the return," he said.

It was a long pause, but Ash did eventually manage a response. And so it went on for a while. Normality began to come back in; at least in what degree it could. Ash even began to count down the weeks till she could re-commence regular schooling; at least for a time. Her and Igneous grew closer together still and eventually her siblings were able to get out and take her with them. Then (rarely but nevertheless) she and Igneous were finally able to go out together. At least until something was found out that never should have been.

Chapter Four
Kat

"I can't believe he dumped me like that," said Kat.

"No cell phones at the table," said Kat's dad.

"I'm not using my phone!" said Kat, "*It would simply ruin the meal and damn us all to hell for eternity for you to due w/o the proper and dignified eye contact,*"

"Oh, right. Just so used to it," he said.

"I just, after all we've been through, for so long-" said Kat, starting to cry.

"KAT! I've had a hard day at the office, Can I not just have one night off from all the drama," he said.

"*How bout I frame you for cheating and leave you to dry out all alone,* Yeah sure dad." said Kat.

"Finally, now we've all heard about Kat's day. How was use'd people's day?" he said, "Marquesa?"

"I got a speeding ticket today," said Marquesa.

"*Really, the man I probably would have otherwise married just left me, and here you are bemoaning a fine*," thought Kat.

"When they stop you, you have to do exactly what they say, to the letter, even slowly explaining your movements-" complied Marquesa.

"*And that's why I didn't want to ever drive. Stop and Grope was bad enough back home; but you pressured me and obligated me to claim to want a driver's license*," thought Kat.

Seeing how upset his sister was while they droned on about nothing Crow blurted out, "Never was an issue on the subways, was it?"

"Solomon! Your mother was talking," said their father.

"*She always is*," thought Kat, who then couldn't help but laugh at her comeback.

"Kat, what's so funny?" said Marquesa.

"Oh, nothing," said Kat.

"You're two laughs away from the floor. Why don't you share it with us?" insisted Marquesa.

"Uhhh, it's an old Saturday Night Live skit about, umm, Non-dairy Floor wax," said Kat, just seeing whatever she could regurgitate to memory quickest, which she then relayed as best she could.

Later that evening in Kat and Kam's room:

"Sorry about earlier Kat," said Ash.

"Oh, it's ok Ash. Deep down I was pretty sure it was going to happen. Frankly surprised it took so long," said Kat.

"Well, anyways-This move has been hard on all of us. I'm impressed you've been able to keep a long distance so long," said Ash.

"How you holding up?" said Kat.

"Well, I have you know who," said Ash, looking for something to say.

"You still want to move back to New York?" asked Kat.

"You know, when I left NYC, I left everything. And I mean everything. I would have given, no, I had nothing to lose. I already lost everything. And I can nevertheless hear mom's guilt-trap about how almost all my stuff made the trip. But now. I had never truly had a serious boyfriend. I don't know. If I went back everything I know by now wouldn't be sitting there waiting for me like a closed account on Facebook. But here I have a boyfriend-" said Ash.

"Say, how's he doing. I know you were chatting earlier because I loaned you my-" said Kat.

"Yes, and thank you for it. Ig is doing good. We're growing ever closer, Seemed to be a good strong relationship," said Ash.

"So was mine, not, not that I mean to discourage, just-" said Kat.

"I understand, long distance doesn't work. I doubt they really wanted to break you two up, But I'm sure they didn't care. Why, I was thinking that use' two would probably eventually get married-" said Ash.

"You too?" said Kat, wistfully.

"Imagine if Mom walked out on Dad, and we told him that we'd had a hard day at school, that we just wanted a day off," said Ash.

"Yeah, sounds like something an evil judge would do," said Kat.

Kam walked in.

"Hey, what about you?" asked Ash.

"Yeah, what about you?" asked Kat.

"Who wha-now?" said Kam.

"How you still taking the move?" asked Ash.

"Oh!" Kam paused to answer and then said "Better than our brother."

A paused filled the room for just a moment.

"Oh yeah," said Kat.

"The guilt he must feel," said Ash.

"I've tried telling him-" said Kat.

"Mom and dad claimed that it was career-" said Ash.

"A likely story," said Kat.

"Yeah, I know," said Ash.

"You know who I really feel sorry for?" said Kat.

"Who?" said Ash.

"That girl on the internet," said Kat.

"Going to have to be more specific," said Ash.

"Now you sound like Mom," said Kat, then seeing the look on her sister's face "*Oops* sorry. That was in poor taste. Who I was thinking of was the girl who said how he made her do chores so he'd be on his own when he was old and sick. Basically he will have already gotten work out of her, and will have blown it," said Kat.

"Yeah, I remember that. Didn't she basically later say she agreed with him on having shot her laptop, and they were closer?" said Ash.

"*Now you **really** sound like Mom*. Yeah, but it's probably like us and our parents interests. Around it enough, being brought along enough we come to like it and eventually sometimes prefer it" said Kat.

"No, in hindsight it's probably just what she's obligated to say. Deep down she's in solitary confinement," said Ash.

"But, it could happen to anyone. Just one comment that he disagreed with, just one that crawled up his blue jeans," said Kat.

"Yet, you know right about know he's one of them that's babbling on about snowflakes," said Ash.

"Ooo! Do not say that word! Get enough of it from Mom and Dad!" said Kat.

"My bad," said Ash.

"No, problem, it's ok," said Kat, "Yeah, just, it was just so, so-"

"Final?" finished Ash.

"What's final?" asked Kam, "Or is it any of my business?"

"The girl who had her father from IT, shoot her laptop," said Kat.

Kam then said a word that cannot be repeated.

"Careful, history will repeat itself if Dad or Mom hear that," said Ash.

"And admittedly it is not the best," said Kat.

"What? Was that out loud, you heard it?" said Kam.

"Fraud so," said Ash.

"Oops," said Kam.

"It's ok, we're your family," said Kat.

"No, your my *Siblings*, family-" said Kam looking for the words.

"Yeah, don't remind us," said Kat.

"Yeah, I can see how that story could be haunting," said Ash.

"Oh, it doesn't out-right haunt me. There are cases that do, but that doesn't truly haunt me," said Kat, "It simply, well, one comment, just ONE, one that didn't let him be absolute and final judge. And that was that," said Kat.

"Yeah, that, I-I can see where you're coming from," said Ash.

Later the next day at school:

"Please, we can work this out," texted Kat.

"No! This just can't work," replied her now ex.

"Please just move on,"

"And stop texting,"

"Ahem!"

"Oh! Uhh, hello," she said.

"No cell phones on school grounds," said the bureaucrat.

"*Oh bug off*," thought Kat as the quickly put her phone away.

"I'll have to confiscate that-" he said.

Suddenly she was in a very bad place, and didn't know how to get out. And while this may seem like a mellow-dramatic mock-epic, she knew how her parents would simply have a cow. She did have friends, and a social life. Just not in the physical world; no that was stolen in the move. Furthermore her ex-boyfriend had been the love of her life. She knew they'd be a great match. He was the only one that made any real attempt at staying by her through it. She desperately wanted to save things, but she knew if it wasn't anything fast, then she would be the dreaded and preverbal crazy ex-girlfriend "Mister, I'm desperately trying to,"

"Save me the sob story, and hand me the phone," he said.

"But, I'm-"

"Now, ma'mm," that little overly polite comment made it clear that she was powerless to even get a word in edgewise. He as an atomoton, compliant and would always do whatever he was told, everything in her screamed and cried to set her foot up on a hot date with his genitals. But she knew there was not talking her way out of it. He wouldn't even listen, without use of a gag. No amount of anything could justify the breaking of rules. She imagined he would make a great juvenile jailor, or at least one that's good at their job.

"Thank you, now for $15 you can have this returned to you, tomorrow," he said walking off with her phone.

Kat was right. Kat felt robbed; there was virtually no chance of being able to fix things with her ex, because bugging him again was all she had left. And her parents would nessacerally side with the school. She was scared, she could lose all access to the outside world, and dealing with people that could only see black and white. Unless she could work it into their world-view-paradigm. She tried to shake her head clear. She'd be called a snowflake, and demanded, treated by people that couldn't listen to the other side and were too smart and mature to be able to be wrong. It would be hurtful, and they wouldn't care. Her pain was nothing but a nuisance that they shouldn't have to deal with, she'd do her best to keep it under wraps and they'd call her a secretive liar. She wasn't cooking this up, wasn't the first time.

Later at home:

Kat was right.

"Don't you see what you're doing to us?" said Marquesa.

"*You've just using guilt as a weapon to get what you want,*" thought Kat.

"What made you think it was ok to break the rules?

"*Strawman, nice*," thought Kat.

The argument, as you would probably imagine, had been going on for some time. Kat didn't dare say what she meant. She, like her siblings, were by all rights liars. Their parents didn't know them as well as they thought. Instead they simply said what they felt obligated to say, what they knew their parents wanted to hear. Sometimes they were really in a lurch because they knew to lie; and didn't know which way. Sometimes they guessed wrong. And as such Kat lived in fear of her comebacks slipping out.

"Answer me!" he said.

"And answer me! We clothe you, we put a roof over your head. Everything you have comes from us and this is how you thank us!" said Marquesa.

"*Yeah, everything comes from you, I depend on you fully. That way you have total control because you can simply take it away because it's legally yours.*"

"Well, I think the school had a good idea, we're not paying for your phone back. In fact I think it's good if you unplug," said her Dad.

Kat felt completely and absolutely overpowered. Her social life and her links to the world were being cut off. And it meant nothing to them. They either didn't know or didn't care what that meant for her. Probably both.

Later:

"Hey Kat, how'd it go?" asked Kam.

"Hurtful, and dangerous, like getting chewed out by your boss at work," said Kat.

"Yeah, I remember having to tell Mom and Dad about it after I got a pink slip from Geary at the Cheesecake Factory in Macy's," said Kam.

"Yeah, that really sucked," said Kat.

"Yeah, so they ground you?" asked Kam.

"Yeah, had to turn over all my electronics. Hoping to not make things worse I just gave up and complied," said Kat.

"I hate that word," said Kam.

"Yeah, me too. But I have a plan," said Kat.

"A plan to make people stop saying 'compliance'?" asked Kam.

"No! A plan to get my phone back," said Kat.

"How? He's too dogmatic," said Kam.

"Dad yes, but the school district, well, them also. But-" said Kat.

"How?" asked Kam.

"As much as I hate to give in, I'll pay the ransom," said Kat.

"I thought that they said never to pay a ransom, because they then have no reason to keep them alive?" said Kam.

"It's not officially a ransom, it's a smartphone, not a person!" said Kat.

"I thought it was funny," said Kam.

"Womp, Womp, Womp, no. And I hate to give in, to submit and feed the beast. But, I don't want to just give them something worth 100s of dollars," said Kat.

"So does this mean you won't need secret internet access from me?" said Kam.

"No, it doesn't. But as it is you're allowing Ash to be close to her you-know-who. And Crow to have room to breathe. And with me out of commission, your workload just doubled. I'll do as little as possible. It will be hard. I think I may even stay off social media in case there watching," said Kat.

"I know you've been doing limited social media out of straight fear," said Kam.

"I am so tired of living under surveillance, having to watch everything I say. Everything I do," said Kat.

"You too?" said Kam.

"Yeah, course you they have chemical infiltration, to appease the school," said Kat.

"Yeah, I-I begged and grovel and lied and compromised. Nothing! I wanted him to file a lawsuit against the school district. Thank you for being there afterward," said Kam.

"Yeah, you ended up having to apologize exactly to his liking, regardless of truth-" said Kat.

"Don't remind me, I mean that. I still hate that. Anything but full and absolute acceptance of blame is seen as simply making excuses," said Kam.

"Just chopped up a bunch of white pieces and black pieces chopped and mixed them up hoping to get away with something," said Kat.

"Stop being here for them, taking their place. Also I'd like to shove those white and black-" said Kam.

"Eww, this is your parents were talking about," said Kat.

"Fair point," said Kam.

"Mind if I go get some Yoplait?" said Kat.

"Nah be my guest," said Kam.

The next day:

"KAT O'Farrell! Come here a minute," said her dad.

"*Only a minute*," thought Kat as she was getting up to go respond.

A moment later:

"What took you so long?" said her dad.

"I came when you called?" said Kat.

"You should not have kept me waiting," he said.

"My bad," she said.

"I hate that *my bad*, say you're sorry!" said Marquesa.

"*I did, I just worded it not to your liking.* Sorry, should have been faster. *Should have run through the house just like you used to tell us not to*," she said.

"I just heard from the school, turns out you paid to have your phone back," he said.

"Yeah, *I paid the ransom*," she said.

"KAT! Don't be rude. It drives a little knife in my heart every time you say that as opposed to simply being polite," said Marquesa.

"In this day in age it should not drive a knife into you every time you hear something *so petty* like that *I should not have to explain this to a New Yorker. Course I guess-*" said Kat.

"UGH! How dare you show disrespect to your mother like that!?!!?" he said.

Fortunately for Kat at that moment Mary started to cry. Neither wanting to be alone with Kat, they went up together to respond.

"*Typical. You talk about how I'm such a good kid, and blah, blah, blah. But when we get into a fight, you say how I only obey when I want to and blah, blah, blah. I have to wonder the truth; but, in the end, I just don't want to know.*" Thought Kat.

Unfortunately, when they came back it was a full on and all out word-brawl. Like many fights it was long and not worth including. But here is an expert.

"You say that you're doing the best you can! But you're doing nothing! Just sitting there like a lump, just making things worse. And with tings you don't know about going on, on top of that! That's the worst possible thing you could do!" said Marquesa.

"You're just plain wrong. Sometimes the best thing to do is to simply remain silent," said Kat.

And with that statement, her mother went off further. She proved her daughter right.

And so it went for too long. But they (metaphorically) sat on Kat, and pried till she said "You talk about what a good kid I am, and how you love me. But when I make a decision that you disagree with-" and with that her parents stopped her; stopping her with a calm that merely thinly-veils a greater anger than mere shouting. A text book example of the calm before the storm. It was different from most fights in that she usually didn't reveal anything! Complete with everything. It was hurtful to Kat; she knew before they'd apologize to her; the Golden Gate Bridge would get up, and dance away. Kat did her best to keep things bottled up. She was grounded into oblivion. Leaving Kam the sole provider of pure internet, and Crow only able to provide limited supervised internet. Otherwise things afterword went back to almost normal. At least for a time. Kat simply worked to accept that that which would have otherwise no doubt became her marriage was simply killed by the move. And it was excruciating for her to accept so little internet. One day she simply needed a little more. Long had it been all balanced upon a shoestring. And eventually, a little leaked out. Hinted at how the siblings were helping each other. Standing together. And it all came crashing down.

And with it; everything else.

Chapter Five

Kam

See the large clock. The Neon that circles it. Watch as the second hand smoothly moves without ticking. Now it's nearing the five. Now it's at the five. Now it's past the five and approaching the 6. Kam had been watching the clock like that for several minutes. Somewhat hypnotically engrossed.

"KAM! Help me carry these drinks!" said / shouted her dad.

"Wha!?" said Kam.

"Now Kam!"

"*Yuck, they need to mop this floor.* I'm on it. *When was the last time they mopped this floor?*" she said.

Kam picked up the drink cartons.

"Come on Kam. Time to go!" he said loudly from halfway across the fast-food restaurant.

Kam hurried out to the car.

"Car-car-car," said her dad afraid.

"*I saw it, I looked both ways. Just you must not have seen me do it,*" thought Kam.

The next dinner:

"Greetings! Welcome to Suppenkuche. My name is Ludwig; I'll be your server this fine day. I recommend the Bratwurst; it is to die for. I also recommend you try our schnitzel. Oh! I'll go get your menus," said Ludwig, who then remembered and went to get the menus.

"He's gay," said Marquesa.

"*Who cares?! In this day in age?!?! I don't think you really have a problem; but if you don't?!?! I mean yes; he's gay. Of course he's gay! Everybody knows he's as gay as Chuck Norris is straight! But why even mention it?!!? Who cares?!!? Shiesh! If you had an issue; why did you drag us all out to San Fran-freakan-Francisco?!?!? I mean it's not exactly known for being macho-land?!*" thought Kam.

"Kam! Take your menu," said her dad; shoving the menu at her.

"Wha? Oh!" said Kam. Kam took her menu.

"*Speaking of gay and macho land. There is that Australian aborigine boy at school. Too bad he's- Oh, who am I kidding. Even if he wasn't he's still be way out of my league. But still, I can certainly enjoy the vie-*" thought Kam.

Crow discreetly kicked Kam.

"For the 3rd time Kam. You want your normal?!" said her frustrated Dad.

"Wha! Oh, uhh, yeah, sure," Kam wasn't sure what they question was, so she just took a guess. With her neuro faculties; that had become a common practice. In fact she had gotten quite good at just having to guess at what people said. Couldn't have people repeat themselves every time that she missed something.

The weekend:

"I mean I should not have to drive all over the city to find your sunglasses! Kam! Now Think! That's an order! Where did you put them!" said Marquesa.

"I'm sorr-" said Kam.

"How Dare you interrupt me when I'm speaking!?!?" said Marquesa.

"*Well when you take such long pauses; how on earth can I tell? That time seemed for all the world like you had finally shut up!*" thought Kam.

"WELL!?!?" demanded Marquesa.

"*Great. Just Great,*" thought Kam (pause) "*Not even a hint?*"

"Now Kam! I will not wait all day for an answer!" said Marquesa.

"Yeah, sure," said Kam.

"Ahem!" said her Dad.

"*Oh great! For once it Wasn't a yes or no question,*" thought Kam.

"I believe that you meant to say 'Yes ma'am'" said Marquesa.

"*If you were any more condescending, you'd pull a muscle* Yes ma'am." Having to submit to an outdated mannerism like that truly was hurtful to Kam. Not that her parents could have ever cared, or known.

"Thank you," said Marquesa, clearly showing her manner entitlement. Then turning to her husband she said "Great, she left her glasses at Thep Phantom after all. Now we gota drive all the way to Japan Center Mall," said Marquesa.

"*But I never went to- Oh, not worth getting deeper involved into this fight,*" thought Kam.

"How should I get there?" said her dad, driving.

"Take Church up to Duboce, than over and up Webster! You're not that new to this city!" said Marquesa.

And so it went for about an hour. Not worth relating that much fighting, also too distressing. It just went on. But there was one note-worthy moment.

"I'm not mad at you!" said Marquesa, speaking just the same as all along, "What on earth makes you think I am mad at you!?"

"Well, I once, fairly recently got in big trouble when you wanted me to take something from you while you were on a step latter, and I accidently raised a voice a moment-" said Kam.

"Oh I remember when you raised your voice to me. But I'm trying to teach you a lesson; are you trying to teach me a lesson?!" said Marquesa.

"*Actually, Yes, that's exactly what I'm trying to do.*" thought Kam.

Later that day,

"For the Third time Kam! Turn the air up!" shouted her dad, "I'm busy changing Mary!"

"I'm on it!" said Kam.

"Kam! You did not change the air filter like I told you to!" said Marquesa.

"*Wow you are so condescending. If you were more condescending-*" thought Kam.

"Hey Kam, What do you think of how I cleaned up your bookshelf. I just go tired of waiting for you to do it yourself," said Marquesa.

"*What!? Great!*' thought Kam as she walked over. "*Ugh! I had them the way they were before for a reason. Hopefully you didn't damage any; but I'm not holding my breath. Great! You basically just made a mess I'm not allowed to clean. Gee! Thanks a lot!* Well, I-I it's nice. Just next time I'd just assume arrange them myself," said Kam, trying to mitigate.

"I'm so tired of having everything I do corrected! You know Kam I really get tired of having everything I do be wrong!" said Marquesa.

"*Oh please!*' thought Kam "*I am so tired of hearing that. I'd need to write it down just to keep up with how many times you've said that just today. Meanwhile almost everything, I do you end up criticizing one way or another. Usually with an addition of something like 'For The Third Time.' Literally! I am so-*" said Kam.

"KAM! I told you to wipe up the bathroom floor! It's still dusty!" said her dad.

"*Speak of the devil,*" thought Kam, who communicated some of what she had just thought ve sa ve the look she gave her mother.

"KAM!" said an angry Marquesa, "Sometimes I think you just listen when you want to; and simply tune us out the rest of the time! AND WIPE THAT LOOK OFF YOUR FACE BEFORE I DO IT FOR YOU."

"*Like all those times you, admittedly doubtful on purpose, had a dopey, upset, guilt-ridden face and I wanted to tell you to wipe it off your face?*' thought Kam.

And so the fight went. Marquesa kept it going on and on. Sure Kam told the lies she knew she was expected to. But that wasn't enough. Marquesa just wanted what she wanted, and nothing else would be enough. Kam, like the O'Farrell kids often would, just tried to keep her head down and wait for it to blow over. But Marquesa kept it propped up. She wouldn't let it go. It was one of those ongoing fights. The kind that can go on for days. And because, in Marquesa's mind Kam hadn't surrendered and complied, it was her fault and Kam was just being awful. Digging her heels down into Marquesa's emotions, unwilling to admit to blah, blah, blah. And so on. But regardless of whether or not that's true. Marquesa sure acted as though it were true. Naturally with a fight such as this it heated up and cooled down. On and off. But despite all the accusations. Kam must have loved her parents, at least somewhat in some capacity. Admittedly fear was no doubt the primary motive; but she really did want to spare her parents. But like a nutcracker, a scientology audit, or a police interrogation. They broke her. They pried till they got what they believed they were entitled to know.

To what can Kam's psyci be compared? It's like a finger torture toy. They harder you tried to pull; the tighter it comes. A similar device creates a similar effect for splicing power lines. But it coming out is actually the intention in this case. You want it out. Contrary to claims her parents had been known to make. Kam did want to talk. Desperately. But she had no one she could trust. And like with a finger torture toy. If you pull hard enough (usually, that is on both sides of the analogy) it will eventually work. But if you pull; instead of getting it to gently come off by going in. It's not that it won't work. But it will come off with a snap.

"*I'm just so tired of having to put on a brave face. To be someone I'm not. To try and, and,*" thought Kam.

"KAM! Answer me. You're sitting there red in the face like a petulant child I'm not letting you up until-" pried Marquesa.

"Fine! I'm tired of just having to put on a brave face! Of having to pretend to be something I'm not! Like if I just try hard enough, use all the tricks, and, and, - *So you won't have to be bothered by it!* And I could just-just transcend my ADHD! And-" said Kam.

"See this is just open dialog. You were so afraid of how we would react. But see, it's nothing," said Marquesa.

Kam was surprised. In time she would go on to tell her parents (most) of how she expected them to react. Lesser matters they would make more of a matter of; as you will see. They would never understand and would even complain when she made a fuss over how little they cared about it.

"How are you doing?" said Marquesa.

Pause

"Kam!" said Marquesa.

"Wha?!" said Kam.

Marquesa sulked a slight amount at having to repeat herself and then said "I said how are you doing?"

"What! Oh, I'm fine," said Kam.

"I know what it can do to hoarders[5] when they get rid / loose stuff. Just want to make sure you're ok," said Marquesa.

Surprised at her mother caring she said "I'm fine!"

And so the conversation went on for a minute or two till, unfortunately Marquesa noticed Kam's body language.

"Kam, I can see that you're upset," said Marquesa.

"*What!? Oh no! I'm not that upset, and you shouldn't know that! Body language is simply a means of shoving your big fat nose into that which it doesn't belong!*" said Kam.

---

[5] Kam openly admitted to that allegation, and had for years.

For a little while Kam would try to shield herself. But Marquesa had it in her head sometimes you simply have to sit (metaphorically) on a child and make them talk. And so she pried till Kam admitted it was a painful reminder of just how much her mother didn't care.

By this point Kam had had full realization of just how badly she (Marquesa) had reacted. Kam had expected one of two reactions. Her parents would be in tearful shock; or her parents would be in denial fueled anger, or possibly in disbelieving fueled anger, or some hybrid, or, or, or. Didn't. In fact by this point (wherein Kam was getting rid of some of her stuff; unrelated hoarding tendencies had greatly let up), her parents had actually reacted worse to her eating the wrong thing for dinner.

"We're home!" said Kam's dad

"*I presumed that when you walked in the door*," thought Kam.

"Sorry you had to miss it. You will love Acquerello when they eventually take you there," said Crow.

"*After that fight. I was glad to stay home; just to get away from Baron Von Pry*," though Kam.

"I disagree, you say Nob Hill; more like Snob hill!" said Kat.

"You're just saying that because Mom and Dad told us to all order the cheapest thing on the menu," said Ash.

"Well, I mean. We lucked out and it happened to be good. But, it's, it's just the principal," said Kat.

"I know what you mean," said Crow.

"KAM," called out Marquesa.

"Oy Vey," said Kam under her breath.

Kam hurried into the restroom, where she believed her mother's voice had come from, afraid to delay.

"Kam!" repeated Marquesa.

"*Oops, kitchen,*" thought Kam hurrying.

Kam metaphorically slammed onto the brakes to keep from bumping into her mother; defying inertia.

"How was this evening?" said Marquesa; honestly making earnest small talk.

"Oh, was good, I guess," said Kam.

"You guess," repeated Marquesa. Marquesa couldn't stand unanswered questions.

"Well, Ended up veging when I intended to get something done," said Kam.

"How was my pot roast second time around," said Marquesa.

"Pot roast? *Oh ****; I forgot,*" said Kam.

"What did you have for dinner?" said Marquesa.

Lying would have only dug her in deeper, "Oh I'm sorry, I honestly forgot."

"You forgot," mocked Marquesa, "What did I tell you?"

After about a minute of conversational dominance; Marquesa got Kam to repeat what she (Marquesa) had originally said. Then Marquesa said "Anything you want to say?" clearly hoping for some sort of apology.

"I'm sorry, ADHD. I just can't keep up-" said Kam.

"Oh don't you even. Every day; several times a day you pull the ADHD card. I'm sick of hearing it! Well guess what! A disability doesn't get you out of a job! Somebody in a wheelchair cannot be a firefighter. If you just used the tricks we gave you then this wouldn't be an issue. Frankly I think that you just use ADHD and an excuse," said Marquesa.

The inspiring fight was short. And like most fight's in the O'Farrell family; all really. Marquesa went at them and they just tried to mitigate. Or hold ground. Often they lied trying to make it better. For most of it wasn't even hurtful. Rather Kam was accustomed; emotional callouses and simply going through life on full and complete alert. That is; that's how it began Until she said "You act as though I can just somehow just try hard enough, be good enough, and use all the tricks and write everything down. Like-like I can just transcend ADHD."

"Well, cut out transcend, and you can," said Marquesa on her usual run through, "If you use the tricks then you can."

Kam, taking a risk hoping to get her mother to simply make sense of what she (Kam) was saying said "So if I just Try Hard Enough, I can just overcome ADHD-".

Kam didn't even get to get to the words "So you simply won't have to be bothered by accommodating the symptoms" before Marquesa cut in.

"Damn Straight," said Marquesa, who paused and then said it again "Damn Straight." The words absolutely slammed into Kam's soul. It showed just how hard-nosed, how arrogant Marquesa truly was. It showed things would be the way appointed by Marquesa, absolutely and completely. Never mind medical science or anything else. Just how final it truly was. And at the bare minimum it was at least as much in how Marquesa said it. Would have been better if it had just been screamed. Really this is a poor description; but neither author just cannot describe it any better. For those of you opening the novel to this very spot it had nothing to do with sexual orientation; but rather a Mother who was earnestly doing the very best she could. Trying her very absolute best to straighten out her daughter. Unfortunately her best sucked worse than Dyson and Oreck[6] combined.

Kam was aghast; she had had extremely hurtful arguments before. But this was in the 1%. Though it would take time for her to realize it to have been as severe as it truly was.

On the way back to her room Kam crossed paths with Ash.

---

[6] Dyson and Oreck, somewhat high-end Nordic vacuum cleaner manufacturers.

"Who did what to you?" asked Ash.

Kam passed Ash without a word.

"Kam," said Ash; avoiding the condescension her parents often gave Kam.

"Who! Wha?" said Kam, ever-so-slightly startled.

"You ok there?" said Ash.

"Who?! Wha?! Oh, I'm fine," said Kam.

"Did they whistle at you like a dog because they weren't willing to allow a delay in getting your attention?"

"*That's not that hurtful. In fact usually it doesn't even click with me that that's what they're doing. Certainly it had never crossed their mind. That simply and merely is the fastest and most convenient way to get my attention*, Hu?" said Kam.

Ash, more willing to repeat herself, said "From what I caught, sure seemed like you took it hard. Not sure the reason, though."

"It's-it's just that. I-I'm afraid I'm losing my mind. My ADHD has already gotten worse than I even thought possible. Nowadays I for real and true fear I'm losing my mind, while I have had accommodations. They seem to think, no, they demand, they order I simply transcend. Never mind what is-" said Kam.

Slap!

Ash had made a couple of minor attempts to interrupt her sister; but then she eventually just slapped her.

"They don't love you! Don't you get it!-" interjected Ash.

"But, but they, they feed us and close us-" replied Kam.

"You don't think they are required to?" said Ask, "By law?"

"But they could adoption us, And they, My phone-" said Kam.

"The phone, they have tracking mechanisms. Back in the Big Apple Crow's phone was pinged, said he'd never trust them again; hopefully still doesn't," said Ash.

"But, beyond that-" said Kam.

"Don't be brainwashed! Children only tell their parents they love them because they want privileges, parents only say they love their children because they want their submission, lover only say th-" said Ash.

"But, if that were true-then-then-why would they spend?-" said Kam.

"It's simple. If everything comes from them, then they can take everything away. You control everything, you control the people," said Ash.

Kam didn't have the certainly as her sister; but still it was a hybrid of enlightening and shocking. Kam slowly walked away to her room, calmly. Soon she arrived. When Kam opened the door the first thing she saw was Kat on her bed.

"Hey, how's it going?" said Kam.

"Bad, don't you remember?" said Kat.

"*Oh no! I forgot,*" thought Kam.

"I was caught speeding one too many times," said Kat.

"Speeding? You? I remember the trouble, err, that you were in trouble. But you, you're a good driver," said Kam.

"There was this drunk; or at least I think he was drunk. Regardless, he was driving somewhere in-between stupid and dumb. So I tried to get away. Well that tattler box Dad hooked up Hum, was it?" said Kat.

Kam shrugged.

"Well, in trying to get away to safety, must've gone too fast," said Kat.

"Couldn't you try to explain to Dad?" said Kam.

"Are you nuts? No offence, but that's like trying to get a non-automatonic word in edgewise when you're commanding officer is going at you," said Kat.

Kam was surprised and slightly ashamed to have even suggested that; she should have known better, and she knew that she should have known better. She was surprised. "My bad" said Kam.

"De, nada[7]," said Kat.

"So now what?" said Kam.

"Well, I've been grounded, and, and they think they can simply unplug me and that then I'll get what they deem a life. But no, by their standards I have next to nothing in terms of a life. Now I simply have nothing. It's like when an old bat says 'you're bored, well I'll put you to work and then you won't be bored.' And shoves a broom in your hand. Uhh, No! You're still bored; just now you're also being forced to work! And the bat receives your labor!" said Kat. Then getting sarcastic she said, "So, how you liking your little slice of heaven on earth?"

"Sounds about right. It's just that, they, it's a death of 1000 cuts. No one particular thing I can point to as the root problem. But every time I have an ADHD moment, they correct me about it. Or at least to me it seems about that bad. And on the instances in which I make and defense whatsoever about it. It's instantly deemed 'one of those things you're always saying' Never mind I could never keep up with just how many times the majority, probably vast, that I hold back. And they have their own stuff they say all the time 'you always say that', 'you just act like you hate us', 'You never want to hang out' err, 'be with us,' and on and on and on it goes. So many things, frequency, and, and, and. My life, and the things they say, whether chicken or egg, or coincidence, probably semi-coincidence, not the point. They've at least, at minimum,

---

[7] Translation-it's nothing

started to be true. My life, just, I-. I can't take it anymore! I just can't take what is my life anymore! I just want it to be over!" said Kam.

Realizing what she said, shock filled quiet, a pause filled the room.

What scared Kam really was that she walked through caution, carefully choosing what to de-classify. What it was safe to admit to. She did it out of fear; and feared letting something simply slip.

"*Wait?! What?! Would I just assume have my life come to a close?*"

"*Yeah, I-I guess so.*"

"*Does that really mean that, putting aside would I do it, would I prefer to die?*"

"*Yeah, yeah, it must, I guess.*"

"*Well, I guess it's official. I'm suicidal.*"

"You too?" said Kam.

After that Kam's life went on. Kam wouldn't have really done it; rather she simply would have instead simply just assumed to have died. Not anything changed in what happened. What she went thorough. In time she'd go in medication. If she had been disruptive the school district would have demanded it a long time ago. But she wasn't. Rather she just slipped off into her own worlds like she was covered with inter-dimensional grease. But the drugs, one was an off label use and intended for people hearing voices in their heads. And they simply put a lid on her; all of her. Thereby making her easier to deal with. With it she was less of a problem, except when it was late and they were keeping her up. The drugs also bore similarities to contraband substances. But her parents were anything but rebels. So they never would have dreamed of rebelling and fighting the school district. Besides that life simply went on as it had been for some time for some time. Some.

Chapter Six

Crow

"Oh! I put mayonnaise on your sandwich. I'm just doing too many damn things at once! Could you just eat it this way for once?" said Marquesa.

"Sure," said Kam.

Crow felt sorry for his sister. He was sure she was smarting off in her head about something like "I know you're allergic, but I'm in such a rush. Could you just eat a pb&j for just this once?" He felt guilty for not stepping in "*Shesh! I acknowledge that you're doing too many things at once. Personally I think you should stop some of them; have Dad just hang up on that guy. But could you kindly give the same pass for Kam when she has the same thing happen. What's good for the goose is good for the gander. I also note you not making any attempt whatsoever to fix it. Never mind how much I know she hates it*" Crow knew that to say any of this would be taboo.

"Do Not Use That Tone Of Voice With Me!" said Marquesa.

"My bad," said Kam.

"I hate it when people say stuff like No Problem, or My Bad. What you should say is 'I'm sorry,'" said Marquesa.

Crow had always had a hard time with reading people; but he was pretty sure Kam didn't realize any violation in her mother's manner expectation. Course; he couldn't be sure.

"Hurry Solomon! Don't miss the bus!" said Marquesa.

"Sure thing Mom," said Crow.

Late in the afternoon that same day:

"So, I hear you've not been so good to your momma," said Crow's Dad in an imposing tone.

"HI Dad," said Crow.

"Is this true?" said his Dad.

Everything in Crow shouted, but didn't scream, to just hang up on him.

"Well, I'm sure you'll take her word over mine," said Crow.

"Solomon! You were incredibly rude!" said his dad.

"Was I?" said Crow.

"YES!" You wouldn't even look her in the eyes! Now isn't that rude or-" said his dad.

"Not in Vietnam," said Crow.

"What are you! A logician?! This is not Vietnam! And no one will look down on you for being polite!" said his dad.

"Sure they would! I might! When people are always saying Sir and Ma'am, it's the opposite of real. It's dusty and starched. It's just blindly and mindlessly following the prescribed rules of politeness!" said Crow.

"So, being polite is just, mindlessness, fake?" said his father.

"Overly politeness; yes," said Crow.

"So you would actually look down on someone for being too polite?" said his father.

"I try not to look down on people; even automatons," said Crow.

"So, are you saying that saying please and thank you is atomotonic?" said his father.

"Speaking generally, no. Not worth going into exceptions. But what is atomotonic is when people are polite, but they use a neo-manner instead of the one you fell you should have been graced with," said Crow.

"So, we should simply get used to people saying 'no problem' instead of 'you're welcome'" said Crow's dad.

"They are saying that; just wording it differently," said Crow.

"Like how you never say yes and no?" he replied.

"I do! Just not all the time. Sometimes I even will say Sir and ma'am," said Crow.

"Almost never!" said his father.

"Seems to me to be every time I turn around. Guess we both see and remember things from our perspective," said Crow.

And so it went on. But as bicker-esque as that may have seemed. That was more open. Than Crow had been in months; maybe years. For all that they demanded information of him on a regular basis. It would seem that simply being able to listen, to not be absolutely grounded in what you believe is right and you absolutely cannot be wrong, that you can hear what the other person is saying. That made all the difference.

Another call later that day:

"SOLOMON!" said an angry Marquesa, skipping saying hello, "I Told You To Put This Bell On Your Bike BEFORE You Left!"

"I tried!" said Crow,

"Do or do not do; there is no try," said Marquesa.

"Yoda was wrong," said Crow.

"I was talking!!" said Marquesa.

"My bad," said Crow apologetically.

"Look Solomon, I want you to have that bell so that you can-" said Marquesa.

ANK!

"Ugh! Just pressed the button by accident. So that you can have a horn; you know that people don't always obey traffic laws," said Marquesa, "Now I want a good reason why you didn't put it on! And I hope you've pulled over, stopped and will come right back quick when we're done."

"For starters there's a tab that keeps it in place, to open the battery compartment you push it down. But it's about to come off, so it isn't holding it in place," said Crow.

"Wasn't busted when I bought it. You opened the battery compartment too many times and caused plastic fatigue, didn't you?!" said Marquesa.

"It was an accident, initially it-" said Crow.

"No excuses!" interrupted Marquesa, "So I bought you a safety feature to keep by baby, you, safe. And you just broke it!"

"Well-" said Crow.

"Yes or No!" demanded Marquesa.

"I can't just give an up or a down; a one or zero answer. Things just aren't that simple!" said Crow.

"You can't or you won't!" said Marquesa.

"Fine! Yes! I broke the Bell-" said Crow.

"Well, it seems that that's not the direction you'd have to press it to sound the alarm; so that shouldn't make any difference. Any other great excuses?" said Marquesa.

"I believe I kinda sorta couldn't-"said Crow.

"One more weasel word and animal control would have shut us down for overcrowding of animals," said Marquesa.

"I tried to put it on! Wouldn't go!" said Crow.

"Handlebar too big?" said a doubting Marquesa.

"Too small! Was on their loose dangling down," said Crow.

"Then why didn't you tighten it?!" said Marquesa.

"I did! Just couldn't be tightened that much," said Crow.

"I highly doubt that," said Marquesa.

That was something commonplace for Crow. Not pleasant, but a daily occurrence. And altogether a fine example of a common fight. Obviously Crow didn't fight with his parents everyday about bike bells. But there was always something. It also serves as a fine example of Marquesa always and only seeing the world in black and white. And being truly unable to see shades of gray.

The next fight:

BAM BAM!

"Ahh!" jumped a startled Crow.

"SOLOMON!" said / shouted Crow's dad.

"Figures! You had your ear buds in again!" said Crow's dad.

"*That's because I want some privacy in what I listen to. W/o your little subtle criticisms as to the songs and genera I listen to*," thought Crow.

By this point Crow had made it to the living room. "We've been calling and shouting for you! Maybe if you didn't have your stupid ear buds in then you could hear us!" said Crow's dad.

"*Well with a phone call you sometimes just can't reach the person! Shieh! Why must you always be able to reach me?!!? Why can't you just sometimes accept that you can't reach me!*" though Crow.

"I see that you disobeyed me in our new program to help you get your homework done quicker. Care to tell us why?" said Marquesa.

"*Oh great! Another not rhetorical question*," thought Crow.

"I'm waiting," said Marquesa.

"Oh, I thought it was a rhetorical question," said Crow.

"No! When I ask a question; I expect an answer," said Marquesa.

"*No, it was rhetorical, you're just plain wrong*," though Crow.

"I'm waiting," said Marquesa.

"I was just trying to get my work done. That's all," said Crow. He was lying; and desperately trying to keep things in tact, scrambling for what to say.

"So why couldn't you just take a moment to write the time in, time out?" said Marquesa.

"You really think for a minute it would be that quick?" said Crow.

"YES!" said Marquesa.

"*Great, here I am wanting to kill myself to get away from you and you're just keeping at it!*" thought Crow.

And so it went on for some time, Marquesa prying and forcing Crow to answer. And while what you just heard from Crow may seem a bit off the wall; it isn't. You see, this most assuredly is not the first fight wherein he "[wanted] to kill [himself] to get away from [her] and [she] just kept at it." Being a reader you cannot feel what he feels; he's been suffering for quite some time at this point. Eventually this fight reaches a conclusion, unlike normal Crow eventually does get the truth pried out of him.

"Solomon, just tell me," said Marquesa.

"Fine! You say that this will help to keep track of how much time I spend doing schoolwork. I say EXACTLY. It's so you can know exactly how much time I spend on schoolwork. So you know just exactly how much time I spend goofing off. So you can know it down to iota and you can have more control," said Crow.

Marquesa was aghast. Some of it no doubt is her lack of exposure; Crow just being untoward what she wanted / expected. She came back with a reply "You're being hurtful at the worst possible time! There are things going on that you do not know about. And then you go off like this!"

"*Yeah, I'm being hurtful at the worst possible time; and there's things that I am unaware of going on. Who knows, seems like when-ever one of us has X, the other soon follows in that unwanted purchase,*" though Crow.

"You are being a-" said Marquesas' husband.

"Up! Bub! Bup! I do a solo," said Marquesa, "Now, what do you have to say for yourself?"

"*Great, I would need record books to stand a chance of keeping track of how many different times you've put me in this hot seat. Wherein I am doing so bad that I want to kill myself; and you're just keeping at it. Giving me questions I both cannot and must answer. Gee! Thanks! How will I ever be able to tell them I'm Gay?*" though Crow.

Now that fight may seem far-fetched, or like a bunch of junk just thrown in, or probably both. But the truth is that you've not seen this because it just doesn't fit really fit into words. It's deeper, more felt, and even less tangible. As for what Marquesa described, her struggle; that was never figured out. This novel isn't about the authoritarians.

What you just read was not commonplace argument. Crow normally wouldn't break down and let her force her way in. But there were others that were out of the ordinary as well. Just days later an unusually major one occurred. Like most, it started out so normally, like any other fight. Crow had just come home from a trip out to a bookstore. He liked horror, not the kind that actually scared him; but rather that which was merely intended to be scary. He watched news programs. Sometimes though it didn't scare him, he could tell that it was scary. Often that was the best parts. He often didn't want people to know what he was reading; though he never could stop them. He carefully put the book away. But as usual Marquesa wanted to know what he got. She was just curious. He showed her.

"Oh, well, You're bordering on an adult. I won't censor your reading. If you were younger; I'd simply say no...

And so it went. Crow tried to smooth things over; he had been afraid to bring it home; a few books he ended up simply deciding to not read simply because it wasn't worth how he knew his parents would react, or at least feared. Sometimes he was wrong; sometimes he was surprised the other way. In time it escalated; with Crow just wanting to not have to go through the mud that is the bickering. It was longer than it needed to be and generally not worth relating. Except as it went on.

"Fine then! I'm telling you to read it!" said Marquesa, "Never mind that boy I mentioned[8]"

"Fine then!" said Crow.

"I won't interfere in what you read, I won't interfere with your life. I'll just shut up-" said Marquesa.

"*Could you do that a little faster?*" said Crow.

"Is that what you want?! You just want me to just shut up and be quiet?!?!" said Marquesa.

"*YES! Not absolutely like you're broad brushing. But yeish!!*" thought Crow.

"Solomon, what is the deal?!?! I mean really," said Marquesa.

"I'm sorry," said Crow.

"That didn't answer my question," said Marquesa.

---

[8] Most of the argument was unpleasant and not worth relating, "the boy" was a relative of someone Marquesa knew from church. His life fell apart and he had read some horror novels. Allegedly that was at least part of it.

"Oops," said Crow, "*ut oh.*"

"Solomon, just tell me!" said Marquesa.

Crow thought "*I am just so tired of having to put on a brave face, like in the Latuda commercials and then face the day. To pretend to be something I'm not. I'm just so tired.*"

"Just got Mary back-" said Crow's dad, joining back in.

"Hold on, Solomon was just about to answer me; weren't you?" said Marquesa.

"Alright fine! I'll tell you! I feel as though I just have to put on a face; and be something I'm not! I try and I try; eventually I start to give up and you see what happens. And also I just fail to be able to force myself to be that perfect, adoring son you always wanted, I begin to feel guilty. Like I could if I tried hard enough," said crow. Crow had many secrets; however that may have been his biggest. Though he did have others. A Gay, in San Francisco. Imagine that. That's not a clesea at all. Honestly he had been like that probably all his life, telling a small smooth-it-over lie as a small child. Almost always worked. In time he'd simply want to want to tell the truth. Simply didn't like to lie. Years would go by and eventually this would come up. He'd get secrets, they'd get bigger. But contrary to what Marquesa would go on to say (not within this narrative); every single time there was a problem with his secrecy, it was solely caused by him not being able to keep it a secret. Weather from an internal or external (parental) causation. This was huge. He had kept it fearing their reaction, but also the earnestly wanted to protect them. He may not have felt love for them; but he didn't want them to go into that sort of pain he knew they'd go through, realizing what they put him through. Or they'd be furious, whether in denial fueled anger or simply the anger of being hit with a slander. He was so wrong.

"See, this is just open dialog," said Marquesa. And as such the fight fizzled out. It meant nothing to her. Not at first; but in time Crow would soon realize, short of notable physical abuse, that was the worst possible way she could have handled it. That was a new height. Like most O'Farrell Kid's fights; it would be later that the true extent of it would later be realized. Heights they simply would never let it again reach.

Meanwhile in the meantime:

Marquesa came up to Crow and tried to put scrunches in his hair. It wasn't long enough for just one.

"Hey!" said Crow, "*try as you might; it's not long enough for you to be able to do that!*"

"Just trying something on my son's long hair," said Marquesa.

Crow's dad laughed.

Last time Crow had had a haircut Marquesa said, right after they had started trimming, that if he wanted to let his hair out to just let her know. Well the next time haircut time rolled around he simply said that he wanted to put it off.

"Hey, you're the one that wanted to let it grow long," said Marquesa.

"Come on! It's not that long. I wouldn't even want it to be that long!" said Crow.

"Well I think it's a mistake; but it's your hair. We're heading out to Mijita Cocina, There's plenty of food in the fridge," said Marquesa.

"I'm sorry?" said Crow.

"Hey, you be seen in public with hair like that, everyone will think that you're gay," said Marquesa.

"*It's not a gay thing! It's not! Furthermore so what if they do?! Even your friends from mass wouldn't be bothered, some of them have been gay. I mean it's not like were in San Francisco or something.* Oh I don't know; long hair isn't nessasarally feminine. In fact it can be masculine. *If I wasn't I'd still want it.* Si Robertson has a pony tail; all those guys have long hair, just look close," said Crow.

Marquesa replied "They also have long hair coming from in their chins. Now unless you want everyone to think you're gay..."

"Ok, sure thing mom," said Crow.

"Now, would you like for me to pick you up anything?" said Marquesa.

"Yeah, how about a pork taco," said Crow.

Often Crow would see someone with longer hair, and even except it to be a man. More-so sense arriving it The City. Among other things Crow would go on to point out that because his hair was just longer, and that Marquesa had basically said she didn't want to be seen in public with him, but that there was the most that ever came of it. They never truly fought over it. In a matter of days Crow decided that it was easier to simply give up and go with the haircut that she wanted than listen to her go on.

Later:

"Solomon! Could you come help me set the table?!" shouted Marquesa.

After a pause Crow replied "Sure Mom" and jogged in.

"Put out paper napkins, knife, fork, spoon," said Marquesa, "And drinks."

Crow got out the napkins and silverware.

"Solomon, did you set the table for dinner?" said his dad walking in.

"Yes sir," said Solomon.

"Napkins, knife, fork, spoon, drinks?" said his dad.

"Napkins, knife, fork, spoon, dri-" said Crow.

"You forgot," said his dad.

"Opps, my bad," said Crow.

Crow walked back into the kitchen, carefully and quietly releasing a sigh though his nose.

"What's wrong?" said Marquesa.

"What! Nothing!" replied Crow quickly.

"Really? What's wrong?" said Marquesa.

"Nothing! Nothing's the matter," said Crow putting down a glass and going to fill another.

"Solomon, I can tell that something's the matter, just tell me," said Marquesa.

Solomon had been thinking about the girl, probably you remember her from some time back, made one comment on the internet about her chores from her dad. And he literally shot her computer. He thought about it and he thought about it and he thought about it. That was that. No appeal, no process of appeal. No reduced anything. One comment wherein people that weren't him or those he knew would back him up would remoteestly be brought in. It was just so, so final.

"SOLOMON! Answer me!" said[9].

Stuff like that had bothered Crow for some time; though much longer than they had been aware. Crow knew he needed professional help, but talk of that lasted exactly one evening; he couldn't risk questions. It started out what they did to his friend Catr. But has sense spread to include related matters

(Insert picture of the Golden Gate Bridge here)

"Get back to the subway platform NOW; that's an order!" said Marquesa.

---

[9] Need it be typed?

At this point Crow had been sneaking around, getting involved in sub and counter culture. He had made friends and had established himself in the gothic community of the big apple. And at home it had been escalating.

"I SAID NOW MISTER! How do you even propose getting in?! A fake ID!?" said Marquesa.

"Go away," said Crow.

"If you go in there I will ground you for a, no, 2 months," said Marquesa.

Crow froze, he knew what would happen if she had victory this time. At the same time if he had the gaul, the audacity to prevail over her...

"You can't-" said Crow "How-how did you even find me here?"

"Oh please, I got an app and pinged your phone," said Marquesa.

That scared Crow, being under surveillance. A surveillance that would not soon end.

"Come on Crow!" shouted one of Crow's other friends.

"This is Not where you belong, trust-" said Marquesa.

"Trust you?!!? How can I ever trust you? You pinged my phone," said Crow.

Marquesa grabbed Crow and started to drag him off. And he knew what would happen if he prevailed her physically. It was demeaning and looked like he'd merely be the demeaned laughingstock of the day. Then Catr came in.

"YOU! STOP!" screamed Catr.

"Get away from me or I'll- oh the police is right there," said Marquesa reaching for her phone.

Catr grabbed her phone, she tried to yank it away, he pulled it from her grasp.

"Thief! Robber!" shouted Marquesa, as Crow managed to get away. Then she started hitting Catr and he backed off for the moment.

By the time Marquesa caught up with Crow he was halfway in the door.

"Ahh!" said crow.

"Well, it seems that I just can't stop you!" said Marquesa, realizing that that boy (Catr) had just popularized defending Crow. Crowds were beginning to from; hostile crowds that might take her on. So she thought she'd try to undo Catr's work. "But you simply can't be seen in public like that!"

Marquesa began the timeless and obnoxious as ever routine with a napkin like should only be done to a small child. She thought maybe she could force him out if the sub-culture vis-à-vis[10] humiliation.

"Stop it stop it," said crow discreetly, who then said more audibly "Mom I'm just trying to fit in!"

"Oh, I know," said Marquesa, verbally smiling.

Catr previously thought that fighting his friend's battles would be an embarrassment. But as Marquesa gave that last, and honest, comment. He began to hear chuckling. Catr had his own previous experiences and, for better or worse, wasn't going to just let it just happen again to someone else while he just sat around breaking wind. He ran up. Catr grabbed Marquesa and pressed her up against a wall. He read her the riot act and gave her a good what for. He said everything that Crow was afraid to say; he really did lay out a good argument, though not documented. Marquesa got scared. She was doing her best to do what needed to be done; the *"tyranny sincerely exercised for the good of its victim." And in that moment Crow broke through. In that moment, albeit by brute force, was an authority higher, above that of Marquesa. She even had to worry about herself! Thought she ended up walking away with only minor scratches on her face and both mentally and ideologically well shaken. She did believe in turning the other cheek and forgiveness. But the way she handled that was a greater hypocrisy than that of a televangelist throwing brimstone at sexual immorality. Catr had been in trouble*

---

[10] Translation- By means of

with the law before, and she saw to it that he was locked back up. Didn't even listen to what he had been through before, to her it was all blah, blah, blah to her.

(Insert picture of the Golden Gate Bridge here)

One week later after that they were in the City by the Bay, and no hope of going back. Uprooted from everything physical. Left with only the digital, course if you're only going to have the digital, San Francisco is the city to be in. Sure his Dad claimed it to be career related; but would have had about as easy a time to convince them that he was moving them to have an affair with the ghost of Virginia Woolf[11]. Crow, sure he had transplant shock. But he really ended up seeing what his siblings went through. Knowing his friend must have been going through! And from that it was all sorts of similar / related issues. They bothered him, ate at him. And when he did happen to let up, he felt some guilt in that he felt like "with all there going through, and here I am getting my room redone[12]." So bothered was Crow that he eventually realized he'd just assume commit suicide, just so it wouldn't bother him anymore. But besides the concept of taking your own life because of how bothered you are about what's happening to someone else, or even others. He did have morals and didn't want his parents to go through the loss of a child. For some time this went on, and all his life, at least to some degree, he had had to put on a brave face with his parents; but it eventually got to where he might actually do it just to get away from them.

"Solomon, why won't you just answer me?" said Marquesa.

"I said it was nothing! It just is!" said Crow.

---

[11] ABSURD!

[12] At one point he does get his room re-done, but it doesn't come up again.

"You know, sometimes you get on us for not reacting to something, other times you get pissed for what we do do. Could you please give us some guide as to when we should react, and when we shouldn't," said Marquesa.

"*Sure there have been times that I wanted you to react; but oh well. However it's a good starting point to have a reaction, even a bad one, when I tell you a deep dark secret I'm suicidal over.*" said Crow.

By all rights Marquesa was showing off her ignorance. Crow understood that she would never be patent enough to listen to him explain what truly did separate now and then. And even if Crow did explain she would no doubt see things from her perspective so badly she could - never make sense of it. Furthermore Crow was afraid and kept secret trivial and inconsequential matters out of fear. He would never dare or dream of that much detail.

"I have raised you. I have fed and closed you. I have provided for all your needs; Don't I Deserve To Know?!?!" said Marquesa.

Crow, as always, did eventually say something "Why do you have to know? First of all body language is not a scientific as you suppose, you're not always right. Second, sometimes you are right; that's worse. I live in fear and try to hide things, I work so hard at it. Not that you'd ever dream of appreciating it. But sometimes, it just slips out. It just does. I can't control my face or I slip and speak to you in the wrong tone of voice. TONE Body language is just a way to jam your big fit nose into the sanctuary of someone else's mind. It's disturbing and violating!" said Crow.

As if she hadn't been hurtful enough this was the first time Marquesa went on about "Putting on a face. Utterly clueless, not even knowing really what she's talking about. To some her saying that would be something. So shocking that they'd, in shock say to never say again, like some monumental, unforgivable sin. You know what's being described.

Later on:

"Solomon just tell us!" said Marquesa.

"We've been here for over an hour! Son just say it already!" said Solomon's dad.

"There's nothing to say. There just isn't," said Crow.

"Yes there is! You get close, then you stop yourself," said Marquesa.

"*I work very hard to come up with anything at all. I'm pulling teeth to form a response because there is none to be had,*" thought Crow.

"Please, just say it," said Marquesa.

"There is nothing to say! There just so badly is nothing, absolutely nothing! I mean nothing what-so-ever," said Crow.

"This is just verbal masturbation," said Marquesa.

Crow was shocked, sub-stunned by her saying this. It was obscene, and incestuous, and absolutely disgusting. Even if it was some sort of technical term. Few times had Marquesa ever said something so over the line before, fortunately she never this it again. But Crow would from here on out live in fear of her saying that. She also went further; that is she explained just how it was (too filthy to repeat). How he just going over; and over it made you feel good, but accomplishes nothing. (Also showing how she absolutely wouldn't move off ideological dead center; and he simply had to be the one to do it.) Like most horrible comments from her it's after the fact that one realizes just how horrible it truly was. Later Crow came to understand this. He said he'd never allow her to take it there again; because next time (he would have done this that time had he been enlightened to the extent that time) he would simply look Marquesa in the eye and say "I think you should leave; I don't think you should come back tonight"

Chapter Seven
The End

"So, this is it. This is the end," whispered Ash.

"Guess so," whispered Crow.

"Done," said Kat.

"Shhh!" whispered Crow.

"Don't want to wake them," whispered Ash.

"My bad u'se," whispered Kat.

"Waja find?" whispered Ash.

"Well…" whispered Kat.

"Come on, what do you have to fear from us?" whispered Crow.

"I, I just couldn't resist. I went into my Facebook page-" whispered Kam.

"Meh," said Kat quietly, half trying to stay awake, half trying to go back to sleep right there in the chair.

"It's ok, we understand," whispered Ash.

"I began to get caught up, at least as much as possible. I came across this guy," whispered Kat.

"Ut oh," said Ash and Crow.

"No! no! Not like that. He's planning likewise; and we talked for a bit. Then we went off to do research as I should have-" whispered Kat.

"De nada," whispered Crow.

"Well, afterward we texted back and forth. We came to the agreement that carbon monoxide is the most painless way to die," whispered Kat.

"I've heard of that, you just, assuming it does kill you and you aren't saved that is, you just fall asleep and never wake up," whispered Crow.

"I would've thought an overdose, like a drug overdose. If you're going out, might as well have some fun in the process," whispered Ash.

"He's had issues, not certain enough would be enough. And certainly not willing to risk a sting," whispered Kat, "I wondered myself why not simply a non-illicit overdose. But he thought that was how women killed themselves and he didn't want to go like that."

"Wait, wai, wa, why is our deaths and his inner twined?" whispered Ash, "Why can't we and he go in different, unrelated, ways?"

"Because he lives in the Tenderloin; and he's going to pick us up in the morning; we'll just leave like we're leaving to wait for the bus as per usual, then walk down to the corner with the broken hydrant," whispered Kat.

"That's several blocks away; why the extra walking. Won't need the exercise?" whispered Crow.

"Same reason you always make a right turn out of the driveway on bike rides. Don't want them to see anything they don't need to. Even at that, might want to see if we can be out the door early" whispered Kat.

"Wouldn't we want to be late; so they won't see a void of us?" whispered Crow.

"Less dangerous than having to pass our friends," whispered Kat.

"What a memory that would be," whispered Ash, it clicking with her. "You made the right decision."

"Also wouldn't want to be caught waiting, Well Within The City traffic can be bad. Especially in the morning; And he's going to have to be driving well in the heart of South San Francisco," whispered Kat.

"So, like, we're hailing an Uber of death?" said Kam, waking up.

Ash shussed Kam.

"Well, I-I suppose so," whispered Kat.

"Say, just curious. Where were our phones hidden anyway?" quietly asked Crow.

"Oh, I have no idea and wasn't about to run the risk of waking them digging around; I just quietly borrowed Mom's phone," whispered Kat.

"That's risky, don't you think?" whispered Crow, fearing he was harping.

"Oh don't worry. I'm good with teck. I'll clear the history," whispered Kat.

"Just worries me they might figure it out, and stop us," said Crow, thinking first it was ok. Then he realized that that was the comment that was not be made. His sisters froze up in fear, terrified. The thought of them trying to end it all and failing; the parents panic, rush. The scramble for information; to maintain control of the situation; to get them the help they needed; the hyper-emotional reaction; everything being brought out, kicking and screaming. The restraints. As such he held back on mentioning that they may be walking into some form of trap.

The next morning:

"Here it is," said Kat.

"Guess I had no real room to complain about the extra waling after all," said Crow.

"When do you think he'll pick us up?" said Kam, "After we passed the bus stop; were all bare / exposed."

"Shouldn't be long," said Kat.

"So, this is how it all ends. I always thought that I'd be a chalk outline," said Ash.

"I'm not terribly surprised," said Crow.

"Really?! Why?" said Kat.

"Oh, well-" started Crow.

"Crow, I'm not them. It's all moot. There is no more reason, no more need to put on a brave face to let them see," said Kat.

Crow was very surprised.

"Yeah, I knew. I'm sorry-" said Kat.

"You actually understood!" said a surprised Crow.

"Actually I was able to piece that together strictly from her clueless regurgitations," said Kat, "That must have hurt."

"It did," said Crow.

"Do you think that our deaths will make any difference?" said Kam.

"Not a chance," said Crow.

"You-Well-I-that's not the reason I'm doing it-I-I, still, I would hope, to, make a difference. I know I've never heard of something like this before in my life," said Kam, trudging thought ADHD / ADD to think of words.

"Well, hope springs eternal. But no, might be a news event. Probably will make the San Francisco Chronicle and the nightly news. But whenever tragedy strikes, the results, the changes that are made as a result. They are almost never good," said Crow.

"Well, it was tragedy that created Amber Alert and those nets that stop the hockey pucks," said Kam.

"Yeah, so no one will catch the puck. But never mind that," said Crow.

"Do you think the day will ever come where this issue is fixed, resolved, put a stop to? Whatever, however, that would be?" said Kam.

"Doubtful, maybe someday. Certainly not in our lifetime," said Crow.

Kam chuckled; "Good one!"

"Oh good! I thought that it would be one of those where I thought something was funny; but no one else did." said Crow.

"I don't know. A Romeo and Juliet story I have heard is found in most every culture. That is the parents tried to keep them apart; and it was a miserable backfire. I think on some level society; humanity realizes something's wrong," said Kat.

"I'm with you. I've been seeing little things. Things that I'm not sure were even meant to be there," said Kam.

"Like what; I'm curious. Don't mean to pry," said Ash.

"It's ok. Like on that show that mom and dad liked to watch. That episode where the Canadian ambassador's daughter was just desperately trying to get away from him. She just wanted to go have fun. To escape the bubble. Don't get me wrong; she certainly wasn't perfect; to which I say probably the product of her environment-" said Kam.

"Equal and opposite?" said Crow.

"I suppose so. Don't remember how it ended; but she just wanted to breathe. Sure they meant well, and even the Mountie had made kindly plans to show her Chicago-" said Kam.

"Wait! You talking about that Canadian show, Due-?" said Ash.

"Yeah, that's the one," said Kam.

"At first I thought you were going to mention on Rosanne when the daughter, I think the older one. She was really hurting. She just was tired of her mother running her life, her words. She just wanted to escape. Anyone with two neurons to rub together could tell she was not ok. I don't think the show's script writers intended for it to be an exposition of the human condition. But it was! Against my automatic reactions and better judgment I made discussion with mom about it. What I remember best is her saying in no uncertain terms that she was just some spoiled brat-" said Kat.

"Just needed to get over herself?" asked Kam.

"Like that; can't confirm word for word," said Kat.

"It's all automatic; knee jerk. How we are built; who we truly are," said Crow.

"Precisely, I have heard neurology, scientific work, to confirm what I'm about to say. Deal is; I believe that sometimes, we just see things from our own perspective. And we so badly see things from our own perspective that when we come across something that is absolutely perpendicular to our way of thinking and ideas; we can't make heads or tails of it. It's not that we're closed minded, or simply unwilling to listen, but we are literally physically, philologically, unable to understand it. Frankly, that's worse," said Kam.

"You're not the first person I've heard saying that sort of thing; albeit worded differently. But ultimately the same thing," said Kat.

"Frankly, I think that that's the deal with the issue with 'Snowflakes.' Because, when you stop and think about the implications. What that really means…" said Ash, trying to really convey- and also getting nauseated.

"It conveys a viewpoint well. But the viewpoint it conveys is, well…" said Kat.

Crow nodded, and said "Also another example is how the romantics saw Satin of Paradise Lost[13] as the epic hero."

"Well, when I got forced to read it. Sure seemed that way to me. Course I'm sure it wasn't the author's intention," said Ash.

"Well, I guess it be modern vs-" said Crow.

---

[13] By John Milton

"This case I'm not so sure, could it be that it simply wasn't the author's intension. Or, maybe I'm-" said Ash

"I've seen it firsthand. It's not a pretty sight," said Kam bringing the conversation back where it had been, "But, deal is. I think that that's everyone. I try, err, should say have tried, to not be like that. But, it's who we are. Engrained in how we are built. And, I fear. Just what have I steamrolled trough; because I was unable to comprehend?"

"Oh that's a convicting thought," said Crow.

"Regarding that show Rosanne I thought you were going to bring up when she broke thought. It was awesome. She eventually ran away with the boy she was absolutely forbidden to see, I think to another state. And while our parents may have placed a knee-jerk into us to think that that's a bad thing anyway-" said Ash.

"Not Me!" said Crow.

"No, no," said Kat.

"Nope, they didn't," said Kam.

"Well, I'm gunu tell use anyway." said Ash, "Frankly, if it is bad that's their parents fault. If they had simply let them, I'm sure they would have simply broken up; things to have naturally taken their course. Even our parents have thought similar things; or at least so I remember. Maybe they decided that, that unto every rule there is an exception, and of course you always, at least given it some thought, but. In a case like this; all the more reason. Mom's dad thought that a forced break-up would be tantamount to signing their marriage license; or something like that. All the more reason, all the more instance you don't want to do that! Well, anyway I loved that part. And I remember the parental comments about a real-life instance of something like that,"

"Wasn't some host they listened to on the radio?" said Kam.

"Didn't they say they didn't understand how parents could get over some things?" said Kat.

"Sounds about right," said Ash, "Guess that they just couldn't understand how some parents could get past their child having overcome them."

"But seriously, even I don't want anarchy, or parents to be micromanaged by regulations; but is there anything that you think could even come to pass?" said Kam.

"By all rights we've already taken the first step. In Don Quote there was a boy being beaten, and the wonder blunder stepped in to help him out, not being paid. But, like with eloping 16 year olds dealing with their parents. He had been overcome for a moment; but he just took him away from 'Man of La Mancha' and beat him more so. Just because of-" said Crow.

"Didn't he also get on the boy's superior, or was it father, because he was beating a restrained boy who could not resist?" said Kat.

"Yeah, Yeah I think so," said Crow.

"Well, I guess there is that. Ii know the first child abuse case, he had to be brought into the courtroom on a stretcher, and they didn't even have child abuse laws. Instead it was under cruelty to animals 'Doesn't he deserve as much love as the next dumb beast?' That Dumb Quote thing could never happen," said Kam, who then stopped herself, "At-at least not legally that is."

"I'm sure people would be aghast that this conversation," said Crow.

"What do you mean?" said Ash.

"I mean, the comparisons. Similar things often occur with historical parallels," said Crow.

"I don't follow," said Ash.

"Or me," said Kam.

"Well, deal is it often is taboo to compare things to the horrors of history. That's not to say that it shouldn't be done with great caution, and you should be respectful. But, sometimes, basic structures; they begin to remanifest. It's especially bad with scale triangles," said Crow.

"Scale triangles?" said Kam.

"Yeah, If I'm going to be dead, I should at least get out of unwanted geometry classes," said Kat.

"Not like X=(NOBODY)(CARES). I mean, well, let me give you an example. Some time back; don't even know how long. Mom was mad at me, again. We had a fight. She claimed that I was, well, I don't remember exactly what she said. Deal is, she made out that I was disagreeing and arguing with every single thing. But the weird thing is; it was true," said Crow.

"I'm certainly going to hear you out; but still I have absolutely no clue whatsoever as to where you're going with this," said Ash.

"It was in my head, rarely, and usually when questioned at that, then did I voice my disagreement. Course to her that probably was constant, and to me almost never," said Crow.

"What was the fight over? And was it one where she claimed to simply be concerned for you?" said Kam.

"First one, couldn't tell you on a bet. Second, I think, not sure. They usually were that way. But she was mad enough she admitted to anger. But, I, I kept almost all of it to myself. I know I should have lied like normal and claimed that my mind had really been changed and that I would never claim to have been forced to say that, blah, blah, blah, you get the picture. But the comparison is that I was told to think a certain way; and she was trying to get me to think (not of my own free will) a different way. For my own good."

"Like reeducation?" said Kam.

"Precisely! Yes! Thank you! Exactly like that. But at the same time; not like that. By that I mean it wasn't a horrible thing with blood dripping, and cartilage tearing. Where the parallel comes in was. It was in the Hanoi Hilton that they were forced to think a certain way. Don't get me wrong; I do not mean to demean the sacrifice of veterans. I most assuredly was not going through that, and would never claim to be. Instead I simply want to draw attention to a structure. That is that they believed things were a certain way, and should be a certain way, and that I needed to think a certain way. And they just kept at me till I did; and even pried into the inner-sanctum of my mind. It's not like I'm a victim of one of the great horrors of history. But seeing as I will not see the sunrise again I do believe I have room to complain. And yes, I can see how this speech could be seen as demeaning to the sacrifice of some. Issue is that if we cannot draw parallels to historical horrors. If they become strictly off limits. But then - How can we learn the lessons to be taught by history; let alone learn from the mistakes? And the dangerous part of that is that 'those who don't know history are doomed to repeat it'" – Crow.

"I see what you're saying," said Ash, "I certainly have thought that much of what is going on in criminal 'justice' and the foster care system were horrors of history of our time. And only with the latter are people much of at all aware. But I certainly could see how we could have a lesser horror in our hands. Mind if I explain?" said Ash.

"Got the rest of my life to listen," said Kat.

"Well it was on that show mom used to watch in the day time some years back, just a few. One at a time? No. One Day at a Time! That's it! Well, at one point; and I only saw some. One of her daughters ran off with some boy. They were in a slum hotel; broke as could be. Desperately trying to get whatever shred of cash they could; including blood donation. They were being looked for. Eventually she told her mother where she was; which was her first mistake. She demanded to be treated as an adult; to not simply have her mother checking up on her. She refused and even said the words 'fine then Julie; don't come home' She said (and I believe her) that she, and whatever his name was. We're starting out their lives together. They just couldn't make it; admittedly I think they should have gotten married; even if it was not-legally binding vows said to each other. But, she just gave up, she gave in. I don't know what side the show makers even intended to be on, but I never forgot that. And That Wasn't Even Real! She, and also her sister. They both went on to get married, but neither ever seemed happy or to have a good life," said Ash.

"Call me nuts; but I have had a similar experience. It was on that spin off show Girl Meets World-" said Kam.

"That Disney show you used to like to watch?!" said Kat.

"Briefly; but yes. I remember the last episode of it I ever watched," said Kam, "It was where there was this thing online, like a TV show. Well the mom decided she had to have her, the main character whose name I can't even remember, at the restaurant. Well that was when that thing was on. She just went off and watched it anyway. Or at least she tried. Question just how important it was at the restaurant; because the mom was perfectly able to leave to punish her. Should've gone to her friend's house to watch it. It was one of those where for a moment you think that they would have mercy; she didn't. Just came down harder. We've all had a bait and switch moment like that happen. They just think nothing of it. After she left the room, she was going to break the grounding. Didn't work and she just got harder. At school the next day she had the plot spoiled; don't even know how long she had been following that show. Afterward she and her mother sat down. Maybe the show was attempting humor; but to me it was hyper serious. They were doing all they could to be calm and sit down at all. She simply stated she was entitled to make decisions for herself; the mother was aghast; slammed on the brakes had her repeat it. And also pointed out how her mother handled it when she made a decision that she agreed with; 'but now that I've made a decision that you disagree with' I'm not relating this very well, I cannot regurgitate the true dark-authoritarian nature of it all. Ended up she went to her best friend's house. Wanted her help till she could get on her feet; wouldn't even lend her clothes till she could provide for herself. Came so close to the mother giving in; so close. She submitted," by this point Kam was holding back tears, "In secret she was doing a little with her friends; but she even submitted to her friends. Mother gave in a little so right when I watched it I didn't really see how sucky an ending it was. Just couldn't be bothered to help her friend; to subvert her friend's mother. Not even for the whole evening."

Kat shook her head and said "Wouldn't have gotten me back alive if that had been me; err, didn't get me back alive. I guess I should say."

"I'm sure we're all just nuts! Or at least that's what mom and dad would say," said Ash.

"I don't know; another show mom and dad liked; one character was being haunted and was upset by having been put on the spot with a teacher's question in elementary school. Like something to do with curriculum. Like you normally do! And he was an older teen like us, no offence to you Ash," said Crow.

"What offence?" said Ash.

"And it was really bothering how she put him on the spot like that; at that age. So, I wouldn't knock it," said Crow.

"Why don't you think we see more of this sort of thing in media? I mean even the more rebellious shows, that that would likely be something kids are told not to watch. Even then it pulls that direction-" said Ash.

"Probably, well first off all it, for better or worse, it is beginning to break through. Second, I'm sure they have to take into account if they go too far parents may just forbid them to see it. And also must remember that producers and animators are people with their own points of view, whatever they are, the same as everyone else," said Crow.

"So you really don't think that this could ever be solved? Whatever that would even look like?" said Kam.

"Really, I would hope not," said Crow.

"What!?!?" said Crow's sisters in unison.

"Probably be another horror of history. Think about it, no doubt government would handle it by grabbing up power. And experts, might know a thing or two. But ultimately could and no doubt would make the same kinds of mistakes on a larger and one size fits all scale-" said Crow.

"Like the lunches at school?" said Kat.

"What do you mean?" said Crow.

"I mean that, for me it's too much food; for the jocks it's a snack. And everyone has to take raw vegetables that end up filling up the dumpster," said Kat.

"Exactly! Imagine if all childhood became that! And you know there would also be lots of struggles that would brew between parents and government implementers. And parents, they at least know their children personally, they can customize, they can individualize; and no doubt do. But a bureaucrat sitting in an office or on a committee in the department of discipline and childrearing in Washington, or Sacramento, or Albany or even under the gold leaf dome at city hall; they could compartmentalize. Life struggles become documents or unknown. Meanwhile our parents might see through their good intentions to see what was right in front of them. And any attempt to get closer would no doubt leave us all trapped in a system akin to our modern and horrific foster care system, and or would be a farce and not do any real good to speak of. In the words of the Immortal American Author Mark Twain[14] "A blue jay is as corrupt as a politician."[15] Or at least something like that It's absolutely undeniable that we need parents, shoot babies that only have physical needs met will die, that's the horror of Russian orphanages. And those that survive become psycos," said Crow.

"I never said I wanted to do away with the family unit; just," said Kam.

"I know," said Crow, "It's just that, what government child rearing there is; it's failed! Look at the schools. So much dread of school just because of the bullying, whether they are ultimately unwilling to stop it or merely grossly incompetent and unwilling; I don't know-" said Crow.

"Back home I remember hearing of, and I believe it, students who were hospitalized like that," said Kam.

"I'm surprised that in New York you hadn't heard of murders like that!" said Ash.

---

[14] (pen name)
(usually used in referring to him)
[15] What Stumped the Blue Jays By Samuel Clemens

"So, you really don't think there could ever be something, or possibly a lifting of something else that, instead of lifting away the family unit or simply being a means of grabbing power for some bigger machine, as it has in dictatorships, or simply mandating household-juvenile anarchy. But rather liberates those like us; in our situation? Whatever that even would be? Could be?" said Kam.

"Nice idea; but you have a better chance of Chuck Norris coming out of the closet," said Crow, "Much as I don't want to be strangled to death by-" he stopped himself.

"Are, Are you not wanting to go through with this? If you don't you, you don't have to die," said Ash.

Crow paused for just a moment, then realized what the results of hesitation could be, "No! No, no." Seeing reactions he then said "That wasn't automatic. I do want to go through with this."

"Me and Kam are just past 16. But you. You're only a few months from the clear, 18 years old. Are you sure?"

"I know I'm 17; but I just can't go on any longer, I just can't. And after that fight, that, that-" said Crow.

"It's moot; you don't need to go back to that" said Ash, (pause), "Ever again."

"I've been thinking about this for some time. At first I wouldn't really do it; then mom and dad hit critical mass. I wanted out. I thought about how I would do it if I did; fantasies. Or so I thought. I stopped being able to tell where not-taking-it-seriously-fantasies ended and real planning began. Next thing I knew I had a plan for how I was going to take my life. Multiple times I was left home alone, and didn't even know for certain if they'd come back to find me-" said Crow.

"Wow-I-I never, I knew something was up; Never knew that it-" said Kam.

"Please, for me. Don't beat yourself up. Course, this isn't how I planned it. cest' le ve[16], or should I say cest' le demort[17]. How I planned it was that I would walk to where there was something for me to jump off of. Even know how I'd get there. And if I was in my room right in a big fight and just couldn't get away. I'd get that knife that retired marine Col. gave me; Left side of my neck where the major arteries and veins are," said Crow.

"I thought you had a low pain tolerance threshold, and a fear of heights that felt unsafe, like you could fall?" said Ash.

"I do, but, well, The wind wishing past, plummeting, thought it could be fun; maybe," said Crow.

"Sounds like it's been hard, has there been anything that has sustained you?" said Kat.

"Well, I can think of two main things. Starters there's something in one of Paul's letters in scripture. Couldn't tell you any more than that on a bet. But in it, he was I'm sure more eloquent, and certainly took longer to say it. But he said that when you're a child, though loved, you're basically a slave. And with in loco parentis, and having no higher appeal. Barring only the most extremes, you're under their absolute authority. And that's that. And even that court case you brought up Kam, in the grand scheme of history , is relatively new. Also there was Escape from Asylum by Madeline Roux, that in it's hyper authoritarian, dark, and often parental, well. I could never hope to convey its well; I'm not even sure what to call it. But I do know I kept identifying with the main character in ways I could never have seen coming. I don't know how accurate it is, how well researched. But it sure could make you think. And it's not that there was any one big central gasp; except maybe the first chapter. Rather, well it was spread out throughout the book. I saw writing skill going up through that entire book series; as well getting scarier. Course it's worth noting the scariest parts I often laughed out loud at. 'blank faces!' That really cracked me up!" said Crow.

"I thought that you didn't like horror that was truly scary?" said Kat.

---

[16] Translation-that is life
[17] Translation-that is death

"I don't, but others, well. I remember a review on the first book[18] that said she read it at her desk in broad daylight and it gave her Goosebumps. Frankly I think I'm just hard to scare," said Crow, "And you know; it's funny. By all rights it was, for all they disapproved of my horror books and didn't want me to read them. It was them that got me started on them. It began when they were watching that old black and white 60's horror movie Fail Safe[19]. Deal was that it was about accidental nuclear exchange; so ominous, so realistic, it was something of a horror movie. At least in it's time. I liked the movie so much I went out and bought the book by the same name[20]. At least I think it was the same book the movie was based off of. Anyway, that's where I got off into the horror realm," said Crow.

"Ideological horror, it scares not through gross horrors and morbidity; but rather through realism, something that either is happening or could actually happen," said Ash.

"Something like that; There have been others such as Jurassic park[21] and what he wrote after, arguably Frankenstein[22] was as well; though it was never considered science fiction or anything other than straight up horror. Also there are numerous dystopian works as well. But Fail Safe is the only thing I know of that is classified as that, possibly some dystopian works as well. Certainly it is the hallmark; the cornerstone of the Ideological horror genera," said Crow.

"That's it?! A little bit of scripture and a prequel. Nothing else has been sustaining you?" said Kat.

"Don't knock what you've done for me. It was a breath of fresh air being able to bypass the web access controls. But, while I wouldn't call it sustenance, there has been one other thing I have at least listened to," said Crow.

"Really? What's that?" said Kat.

---

[18] Asylum by Madeline Roux
[19] 1964 with Walter Matthau and Henry Fonda
[20] By Eugene Burdick and Harvey Wheeler
[21] Originally a book from Michael Crichton
[22] By Mary Shelly

"There's this radio show. It's for people like me, people really in need of help. Mostly teens, some young adults. Don't know if it ever helped with anything; but I listened," said Crow, "Were a few stories that I never forgot. Normally it was people calling in having relationship issues; but, not always. One she was being emotionally abused; and like usual all he said was ultimately hang in there, and sometimes also that you should do what you can to not pick a fight, so there will be less fighting. But this one girl, she unlike most. When she was asked if she could bear it any longer, or something like that, she actually said no. he did nothing for her; all he said was all he ever said, essentially, was wait till you're 18 and can move out on your own. Another, this girl he wanted to marry. Her family disapproved. I think his father had bullied her father. He basically said to her father he was going to do to him what his father had done to him. Now it was a bad family situation; and I think her father still had some issues stemming back from that. I'm not justifying what he did; But, And as I recall he got beat up for saying that. Deal is; radio host guy basically said you don't want to be marrying into that family and told him to forget her. He should have gotten her out of that family situation! Run off to elope to another state; and have a body builder or marine or possibly a Kung Fu master on either side of you when you go to pick her up! But, out of my hands, I suppose. Another time there was this teenage girl who had gotten pregnant. Her family was so buttoned up and awful that they actually were going to put her up, err, that is at least how I remember it. Basically he just pointed out what good people there are in foster care. Did nothing, and basically said hope for the best. Admittedly that was the worst. Normally he was good; not always. But; don't want to spend the rest of my life telling sop stories!" said Crow.

"Oy, did you ever try to call in?" said Ash.

"Yeah, but normally didn't get through. Only time I ever even spoke to a real person, all that was accomplished was learning it would be almost impossible for me to get to speak with anyone but maybe a call screener, because they would have to call me back when they were ready; boy was she useless!" said Crow.

"I remember I heard a story on there as well myself," said Kam.

"You did?!" said Crow.

"Yeah, well probably more than one but the one I remember was this woman who was on parole because of an ex-boyfriend that was doing drugs that she didn't report because she didn't know about it. Well, was with another dangerous one, will spare the details of his threats. He was a liar, claimed to be in the mob, was warrants out for him and was making all kinds of threats. She couldn't get away from him because of her parole didn't allow her to flee. He didn't offer to help expose him, or tell her to try to record him, or report him. Did nothing whatsoever, no attempt to protect her, come to think of it I remember having heard others. But not any that were worth remembering; or at the least I've forgotten them," said Kam.

Crow thought that he might be ok, thought of backing out. But, he knew that might interfere with his sisters and didn't want to force them… Also after all that would happen. Didn't want to be there to see that aftermath. Thought, he worried that it was peer pressure, or maybe it wasn't really that bad. He knew his parents weren't all bad all the time; in fact at good times he looked back and wondered what had he been talking[23] about. But never for long. He knew it couldn't have been that effect, or at least so he assumed; he was either in the worst of the aftermath of what was at least one of the worst fights of his life; or if it wasn't over the eye of the storm. He just didn't understand that when people finally make the decision to end it; they do get better. With depressed people when they get a little better, that's actually when you need to worry most; in the full extreme they're not able to do it. Such was Crow's case; though depression not being the issue; having made the decision got him through the fight list night and the morning's extreme eggshells. It would all be over soon.

"Think things would, could, have been different if you had gotten through?" said Kam, a little worried that it might interfere her having said that.

"Not a chance, I'm sure he wouldn't have really done anything. And a major, pie in the sky, lawsuit is the only possible chance of making a difference for me. Emphasis on pie in the sky.

---

[23] Talking not in the meaning of speaking to other people. No he was FAR too secretive for that. It just worked grammatically better than the word 'thinking' did in that context.

Frankly, for better or for worse. Not much that even can be done for emotional abuse, at least legally. I don't know what the law says, but-" said Crow.

"You think this is emotional abuse?" said an unreadable Kat.

Confused and worried at what she was getting to that; Crow said "No, err, I, this, this is,"

Ash stepped in and said "This is this. It's its own thing.[24] 'How much does it hurt to have your arm pulled from the socket? It hurts as much as having your arm pulled from the socket'"

"Yeah, There's Illegal abuses, don't know the law on emotional abuse. Then there's this," said Crow.

"You think someone might write some sort of ideological horror about this? Not necessarily us, but this this?" said Kam.

"There are 30,000,000 books in the library of congress, give or take a stinker. Someone has. Not every writer can be Upton Sinclair," said Crow.

"I know, and for the record I counted 29,999,999. It's just, that-" said Kam.

"It's a paradox. The preverbal case of a Katch 22[25]. You go ahead and investigate the case of a girl raped by a teacher who doesn't want to come forward; the next won't even get checked out by a doctor. You repeat something said in confidence for their own good and even if that is for their own good, you make sure that no matter what happens next time; they will be sure to keep it to themselves the next time. You undermine parental rights and you not only have the camel's nose in the door; but also you have just given more power to whatever regime is in power. At least that is been the case with so many historic dictatorships," said Ash.

"Yeah, I heard outraged political commentators discussing the schools giving out condoms; it was mainly behind parent's back, people were outraged, not wanting their kids to be, well, this wasn't even teens I believe. But the paradox is while that might get some to do it that wouldn't

---

[24] See the first quote in the More quotes.
[25] You'll have to look some of the author's names up yourself.

otherwise; others would simply risk and also might get disease. It's a paradox," said Kam.

"I thought you were going to mention that charity that was giving out those, and a few other more essential things to runaways. Don't remember where, but the police wanted that stopped trying to just grab them up off the streets. But that, I'm not so sure is such a paradox. By that I mean by all rights they're refugees. And what the police did, it only made their dark situation worse; and even if they were up off the streets. People don't normally choose to sleep in gutters for fun; you don't know what you're shipping them back to. Could be worse; could be, well, at the very least I would imagine it's worse to them because they rejected it. I'm sure if we could we would just go off on our own; but that's all that might even await us, doubtful we even could slip away," said Kat.

"If we did we'd be sleeping in gutters, eating whatever food we could find, and hiding in terror of truancy; you know we'd be shipped back home without them thinking about it. Work would be out of the question; same with an apartment lease or anything else," said Ash.

"Yeah remember mom going on onto this letter to the editor. It was this teenage boy who was saying how we shouldn't be surprised at teens stealing. Something about how we want to find work; might I emphasize want, as in trying to get but can't, willing to work. But they weren't wanted. But he dared to say how it's because they like everyone need spending money, so when they can't get any way to earn money, this is just what happened. And oh boy! Because it wasn't the most possible justifiable, that is an adult with a starving family they couldn't feed; because all their physical needs were met! Well, I'm sure there has been kids who stole because they were ashamed and no doubt being bullied for looking like dorks; just wanting to fit in. But even beyond that, well. It didn't register with mom, so-" said Kat.

"Was that the one that ended 15 and unwanted?" said Kam.

"Yeah," said Kat.

"We should have kept that one," said Kam.

"Yeah, but we were all too fearful to ask Mom to let us cut it out," said Kat.

"It shouldn't be a real surprise that there's never been a Jungle[26] for us," said Crow.

"Wadaya mean?" said Ash.

"Well, when you see someone going through what we're going through. See it, you might begin to catch on. But TV shows, I don't think a show could change the world. Movie's a little more likely, but will eventually end up something years old on the idiot box. And you just can't really break down how, what-" said Crow.

"'Just as some situations are beyond metaphor, some events are beyond dramatization'" said Ash.

"You're quoting something; aren't you?" said Kat.

"Yeah, book I've been reading. Good book; but not going to get to the end of it," said Ash.

"Ultimately, it's really an internal struggle. It's how we experience. All this is by in large. But, you can visually show, and chronicle the outward results of our struggle. You certainly can write of the causations. But ultimately; an internal struggle, we can't really express it if we were to try to put into words within our own minds. Like you said; how much does it hurt to have your shoulder yanked out? As much as it hurts to have your shoulder yanked out," said Kam.

"Any last reflections on life? Not that anyone would hear it if you made a great and meaningful quote?" said Kat, "According to Crow's watch, won't be long before he picks us up."

Crow didn't mind her looking at his watch. But he did mind the watch "I don't particularly like this watch. And I never wanted to wear a watch! If we pass a trash can I'll ask him to stop so I- no, it's not a Rolex, or anything really worth stealing. Think I'll just give it to a homeless person; Maybe they'll get some enjoyment out of it. Might as well," said Crow.

"Ash, what about you?" said Kat.

---

[26] Upton Sinclair

"It's like this, to me that is. There is this thing you're not supposed to touch; but whether a good thing or a bad thing; you do. And it's supposed to stay in place, but it begins to swing. Now it's important, or at least so you've been told, that it stays in place so it won't break. You try to steady it, but that just makes it worse. It begins banging back and forth BANG BANG BANG," she said those last 3 words as if they were hammers, "And you try to steady it, but it just gets back and forth faster, thus harder. You try to push it up against one side, for fear of breaking it's supposed to be 'free floating' but at least if it's pushed up against one side, it will have hit it, but won't be bouncing back and forth. But it's just at that very so very coincidental moment that mom just happens to walk in. Her timing is always like that; you work all day at something and she normally just happens to walk in at your quick break time. And by this point you're in something like a death scramble-spiral. And she is so, so, you were just trying to save, and," At this point Ash was conveying to scramble-spiral in her description.

"Yeah, we all remember the story of how you broke mom's-" said Kat.

"Yeah, Yeah, Yeah, don't remind me," said Ash.

"Funny you should use those terms like bouncing, free floating, and that horrible banging. For me, it, it's like this. You have this, this, well, it's great. But it's fragile; it's like a house of cards, and must be treating accordingly. Course I've been known to do leap day decorations that you had to walk past carefully or else the wind could blow them away. It's been there a long time. Which is what you'd want. But that makes it more fragile. Touching it could damage it. And then brovdignagian mom rushes in. Having a fit; a panic of our best interest. And she, she starts grabbing, touching, she's wrecking it and it's so fragile you might damage it just doing what should be done trying to put it back together. Now a piece is bouncing! BONG! BONG! BONG! It's not even supposed to be touched and it's bouncing!! Police would have shot her if she had tried to pry information using a crime scene like that from them, or so I'd imagine. But to me, me, it's, well really it's filth, and it's a kindness she allows it at all. And you're in a scramble one part she's holding a part in her hand. It's so fragile you need her to hand it over carefully. She won't!!! She won't even hand it over! It's how she'll get her answers. Good God She Had to Have Her Answer! THE QUESTIONS ABSOLUTLY MUST BE ANSWERED!" By this point Kam was drawing attention. There wasn't much attention to be had. But what there was she had. Also her panicked scramble-spiral was so great she could no longer be understood.

"KAM! KAM! KAM!" Kat was gently shanking her by the shoulders.

"It's bouncing! It's shouldn't even be touched and it's BONG BONG BONG" the bongs were like hammers.

"Mom's moot. It's moot," said Ash.

That seemed to calm Kam down. She relaxed.

"It will all be over soon," said Crow," and it's funny you should describe it like that, feels like similarities with mine. But Kat, would you like to go first, err that is before me?"

"Sure, for me it feels like. Well, this thing, it's going way too fast. It's out of control. Seemed ok till it was clear it was out of control and there's nothing you can do to get it under control. Sure you could make it even worse, always could cause an accident; but obviously you wouldn't. It's so bad that you'd jump off or out if you could; it's so out of control. No, you can't. You try to jump; but you get caught, possibly loose clothing. It's already an accident now. It's going down and that's that. No stopping it. And it absolutely will take you down with it. And that you tried to jump and got caught; tangled, just a little maybe. It's enough to keep you attached," said Kat who then rubbed her arm and calmly but internally-strongly went "Ouch"

"For me, it's like, there's these two things, running side by side. But not side by side; not quite. You see, they're close, but not quite. And it's small, usually not noticeable. But as time goes on, it, it gets moreso, or at least more visible. And sure the out of line one in getting more out of line as it goes on. And they cross, the other tries to push it back in line. A hint. A reaction. I think... No it should be... You need to return 5 degrees. No go this way. No Go This Way. NO GO THIS WAY. And, and their off by a little, it does increase, and it just keeps trying to get it in line. Pushing! Indicating!-" said Crow.

Everyone could tell that Crow was getting as hysterical as Kam got. Then Ash noticed a car pull up.

"Oh thank God! I mean it's here. Err, that is, I think that it is, here, err there" said Ash, pointing.

Kat got an elbow then walked over. The driver rolled down the window. "Umm hi, are you," Kat realized Rebel wouldn't work, it wasn't a name and he could very well be the only person in the country going by it. Certainly she couldn't just say "Hi there! Are you here to take us to our death?"

The driver realized this and after he thought of what to say he said "Ya'll the O'Farrell teens?"

At first she was surprised both by the man's appearance and the Southernism "Ya'll." She quickly realized this man, who despite having pulled up to the right people at the right time at the right place; she had truly believed to not be the person they were waiting for.

Kat glanced back at her siblings, nodded, and turned back to the driver and said "Yeah, that's us."

He jestered into the car with his head and said "Hop in."

Crow took shotgun, Ash being the smallest sat in the middle of the backseat, with each of her older sisters on either side.

"Everybody here?" said Rebel.

"Everybody planned to come. We do have a baby sister, but," said Crow.

"Wasn't exactly invited?" said Rebel.

"Something like that," said Kat.

"Everybody buckled?" said Rebel starting off.

"Seriously? I'm not very worried about that," said Kam.

"You want to risk being pulled over?" said Rebel, "Don't mean to boss around, but-"

"Ok, fair point," said Kam.

Everybody already was buckled.

Rebel was driving so he only did a quick glance over to Crow when he said "So, you must be Crow. I assume."

"Yeah, that's me," said Crow with a sigh.

"And you in the middle" said Rebel looking in the rear-view mirror, "You must be Ash."

"Nailed it," said Ash.

"And you other two, Kit Kat I presume?" said Rebel.

"We get that like twice a week!" said Kam.

"We hate that!" said Kat.

"My bad, Kit Kim? N-" said Rebel.

"Hey!" said Kat.

"Hey my bad, haven't been keeping up with too much. Been a bit distracted recently," said Rebel.

"I'll say, Look Out!" half shouted Ash.

Rebel swerved.

"Sorry, I haven't operated a vehicle in years," said Rebel.

"What? You didn't realize that that car was parked?" said Crow, "And Slow Down"

"Don't tell me what to-to-oh whatever!" said Rebel "I-"

"Speaking of vehicles, I thought you said you lived in a bay area slum? How's you get these wheels?" said Kat.

"Hertz. Grabbed up what little money I had; got a one day rental. Might as well go out with a bang," said Rebel.

Speak of the devil, at that moment, they hit a pothole.

"Glad we won't be on any freeway," said Ash.

"Tell that to 280," said Rebel.

"Could, And and I don't mean to pry; but. May I ask why you're all doing this?" asked Kat.

"Ever heard the quote 'You can take the inmate out of the prison; but you can't take the prison out of the inmate'" said Rebel.

"No, I've heard plenty of variations, but no," said Kat.

"Really? Never?" said Rebel.

"You bet your bippy," said Kat.

"What's a bippy?" said Crow to Rebel.

"I have no idea," said Rebel shaking his head.

"Sound's weird, stupid, gross, old timey in the worst way. Like something from the granny on a black and white fish-out-of-water comedy," said Kam.

Ash nodded.

"Well, let's just say I've been through some stuff. Really bad stuff. Stuff such that I wish I had done this in my early-to-mid-teens. Recently the last hope of any real justice just fell though. Shouldn't be surprised when you're going to what is basically a charity law firm. But still. Well, this should get the flashbacks to stop," said Rebel.

"You a veteran?" said a somewhat confused Kam.

"Oh no! Could never handle that! Don't even know how they could get though the training; which only gives me all the more reason to respect them. But, guess that's moot," said Rebel, "What about ya'll? Or would you to just assume not say."

"Well, we want to get away from someone, err, some people," said Ash.

"Parents?" said Rebel.

"How'd you know?" asked Crow, everyone was very surprised.

Rebel shrugged and said "Guess birds of a feather, die together."

"Or get dragged off to different sides of a continent," said Crow.

"What? Or was that something said under your breath and wasn't meant for prying pests?" said Rebel.

"I know what you're describing; and no, that wasn't something meant not for your ears. Let's just say I've seen a few things. I have been having to suppress my true inner-self. Sense all that happened I begun trying to hide it, be somebody else. But at the same time the causation has actually been aggravated because I've given up on it. And having been putting on a brave face to perform the proper show," said Crow.

Rebel winced at that and said "Sounds like my not so great Great Aunt Henrietta. Last night I did what I wished I could do that summer I was being made a proper southern gentleman. I called her up, right before I started talking to you Kat, just to tell her I hated her."

"What a phone commercial that would be!" said Kat.

"Yeah, but she's not your, err his mother," said Ash, "And you, you have southern heritage too?"

"Yeah, not particularly proud, but a southerner indisputably. But you Ash, from your voice I'd have taken you to be a New Yorker," said Rebel.

"I am, with pride. Miss it dearly-" said Ash.

"Not as much as me," said Kat.

"So, were you adopted?" asked Rebel.

"Oh no! I remember mom pregnant with her!" said Crow.

"We can still remember the day she was born," said Kam.

"No, they simply moved there for career reasons when Crow here was just a baby. Before our time," said Kat, "Originally deep south. Though on Dad you'd never tell it."

"What about ya'll two? Cat and Cam, right?" asked Rebel, "If we're all going to be together for the rest of our lives. Really should know your names."

That got a slight chuckle out of Kam.

"Yeah, that's us. For me, it's like. Well, imagine you're in a room, the lights go out," said Kam, "You're told just stay still, stay where you are and we'll get the lights back on. You try to move around. 'No no just be good and stay exactly on that spot where you are' You move, struggling through, the darkness is pitch and absolute. You just can't see; your eyes feel closed. Maybe you should stay put; maybe not. But you don't. 'OWCH' You walk into a chair; it falls over 'I Told You To Stay Put!'" Kat stopped. She could tell that the Omni-authoritarian pull of her story was bothering him. Not just mildly, it was seriously bothering him. "I-I-I'm-I'm sorry,"

"It-it's-it's it's ok. I, I just," said Rebel. He wasn't tearful, but rather this was something else. Something serious. "You don't know me. It was an honest accident."

"They're moot. And where you are right about now. They have absolutely no authority over you whatsoever," said Crow.

That seemed to make Rebel, ok, or at least better. It was enough of an antidote that they were able to safely go on down the road.

A few minutes later Crow asked, "So, like. This is a Ferrari, right?-"

"See the steering wheel?" said Rebel.

"I mean, sure, we're not long for this world. But to we have to go straight there?" said Crow.

What? Like you'd like to take it around a little?" said Rebel.

"Well, wasn't going to ask; but-" said Crow.

Rebel smiled, almost beamed, and said "There's doubt?"

And go straight there is exactly what they didn't do. First it was off to Buchanan Mall (and also New People mini mall). The sisters were all temped by the clothes they saw; but if they did buy anything they'd never be able to enjoy it. It was a weird feeling for all of them; almost like walking through as a ghost, though not quite. Visible, able to be seen and to talk to people. But you really couldn't possess anything. And in an area aimed exclusively at shopping! They soon afterword went off to Yasukochi's Sweet Shop. No reason for dead men walking to count calories; so they ate cake and candy. (Yes, that did mess with Kam's ADD). After that they were full, but went off. All around the Bay area, doing all sorts of fun stuff they never got the chance to do and / or were banned from doing. Ash all along could just imagine and even worried about their parents learning of them skipping school. Freaking and them tearing across San Francisco. As such they never went anywhere they normally went. That and what it would be like if the story got back to their parents if they ran into anyone. Then it was off to a late dinner at Coi. Didn't even bother to wait for the server to bring back Rebel's credit card. This caused them to be mistaken for idiotic check skippers seeing as the $1400 bill was too much for the credit card. After dinner they were out late doing more fun things. As much as death is a feared and dreaded thing. This proved to be one of the greatest days they had had in years.

"That was a great day," said Kam.

"Yeah, guess that was because it was unplanned, a surprise so no time to get your hopes and imagination built up," said Crow.

"Like with trips out to malls for you, right?" said Kam.

"Yeah-" said Crow.

"You don't get to go out to a mall very much, didn't you?" said Ash.

"Well, to mom and dad it was every single month. But, ultimately. I knew it threw a wrench into everything and everyone else had the whole evening ruined for them, totally consumed when-" said Crow.

"Not for me," said Kat.

"Well, I mean-" said Crow.

"You mean for Mom and Dad," said Ash, "They were bored to death, and when the decision was made it was usually spontaneous and a kindness, which made you feel bad like you were messing everythin-"

"Yeah," said Crow.

Kat yawned and asked "What time is it?"

"According to my phone; after midnight," said Rebel.

"Guess we clicked over the date on the tombstones," said Crow.

"I still am shocked at you. Not exactly convinced you're poor-" said Ash.

"I only got a one day lease on this place through Air B&B. Rest of over the time had just been bought up so it was cheap-" said Rebel.

"One block over from Webster Street in Pacific Heights is cheap?" said a sarcastic Kat.

"Comparatively, I mean people that are going to have the money to stay here will also have the money for a longer vacation-" said Rebel.

"Or just stay here for a part of their vacation," said Kam, "Come on, tell us we're not breaking in."

"I took out payday loans. Not like I'm going to stick around to fork over the 800% APR. So-" said Rebel.

"Enough to pay for this?" said Kat, "You said on the phone."

"It was within an hour or two of being too late for the website to allow you to book, and I actually had money left over," said Rebel, "Ok, 49¢."

"Think we should leave suicide notes?" asked Kat.

"No, I don't," said Crow.

"Well, honestly," said Crow trying to find something to say.

"You can say it. You think it will be hard enough for them," said Kam.

"Parents?" said Rebel.

"What about Mary?" said Kam.

"Your baby sister, you said, right?" asked Rebel.

"Yeah, yeah, hadn't thought of that," said Crow.

"History is told by the victors, or in this case survivors," said Ash, "Would want her to know what really happened."

"Actually I was thinking, what of her. What if God forbid, she went down the same authoritarian path?" said Crow.

"Maybe, just, just maybe the shock of it all will be, will be for the best for her. Maybe she'll have a better time. Better than we did," said Kam.

"Hadn't thought of that," said Crow.

"I've already made out mine and gotten it in the snailmail," said Rebel.

"Yeah, well, I think we should do that. Come, we'll look for a computer, maybe we can type it out and print it," said Ash.

"Well, you do that, I've been awake beginning to close in on 24 hours, and Starbucks is beginning to wear off," said Rebel, "I will not need the Carbon Monoxide to get to sleep tonight."

"You could go out for more Starbucks, you know we probably could have coffee delivered," said Ash.

"I don't know, I've already had a lot-" said Rebel.

"Not going to have another change for one of their drinks," said Ash.

"Well, there is that. But don't let me forget. I don't want the other people, whoever they are, to have rented this place for so long, however long I was never told. Well, I'd hate for finding us to be their memory of San Francisco," said Rebel.

"Yeah, also we got together what information we could for organ donation, admittedly not much. We should lead first responders to the trunk where I put all that. Also give them notice at a time it will still be viable," said Kat.

"I've been registered for organ donation; have ya'll?" asked Rebel; cuz I'm sure it's too late now.

They just looked at each other. No one knew.

"Hopefully our parents will handle that properly," said Kam.

"Well, I'm going to go look for that computer," said Crow.

"I'll help," said Kam.

"I'll see about printing," said Ash.

"I'll see about whatever else," said Kat.

Later:

No one knew if they should fasten their seat belt. They looked at each other. The silence, despite how it was often described by Marquesa and her husband, was not deafening. Rather, in this instance, thick. No one knew what to say. Ash had led her siblings in a Hail Mary, and they had all said prayers.

"You sent that message to 911, right?" said Crow.

They were seated as they had been when Rebel first picked them up.

"Yeah, yeah, wouldn't want them to have to find us," said Rebel.

"Or worse, not find us, and we accidently take them out like a broken furnace," said Ash.

"Hadn't thought of that," said Rebel.

Ash echoed that thought from her brother. She had put a small warning on the doorknob outside. They had left if unlocked for first responders. But not open to let gas out.

"Don't see anything we can do about it," said Kat.

Kam and Rebel nodded.

It's strange, it's not that anyone didn't want to go through with it. Even all the way. But nevertheless, it's that feeling with the gun up to your head, right before you pull the trigger. Even if you do believe in the afterlife. H.G. wells described this feeling in *The Time Machine* right before he went off into the future. They were certain, especially after the day they had had, having run off, that horrific fight, they were not wanting to back out. But, they did want to procrastinate, at least a little. It was very late, but not so late that they might not be gone by the time the next group of people had arrived. They had already arranged to summon paramedics and police to collect their bodies and hopefully harvest their organs. It was on a timed delay send. Like an author, working on a part of a book, having arrived at a part that has been thought over and about long before work ever actually began on said book. They did procrastinate at least by moments, by rolling down their windows.

"Everybody ready?" asked Rebel.

It was like leaving on a road trip, everyone had even used the restroom, to make sure nothing happened post-mortem (can actually happen). They were seated in a car. But the car wasn't going to go anywhere, the garage door was closed. It wasn't even going to be taken out of park.

Everybody kinda affirmed. Everyone had some stuff they considered saying; but they weren't even sure if they should say yes. They all knew anything they said would surely be the last words they ever spoke. A slighter but similar air had hung over breakfast earlier that morning; parents didn't notice. It bore a similarity to the post-fight eggshells they had wherein no one would really make any unnecessary communication, so no particular / additional suspicion had been raised.

Rebel turned the keys, turning the car on. "Here we go." And with that; that was the last words any of them would ever hear again.

Ash looked and saw her siblings drifting off. It was well late into the night, and as such, despite the coffee. She wasn't sure if it was that or the engine. Rebel hadn't slept in about 24 hours. But not her. She struggled to stay awake; she worked to keep her eyes open. They would find her with her eyes open.

Chapter Eight

Notes

Suicide Note Left on the front door of - -'s Pacific Heights Residence for Firemen, Paramedics, and Police; Removed By Igneous Belvedere

WARNING Grave Carbon Monoxide Threat. Enclosed are 5 corpses in the garage. THE CAR IS ON. Please remove quickly to recover donor organs.

WARNING

Suicide Note placed before the front door of Pacific Heights Residence (Interior Side) as instructions for first responders; general and Rebel Lombard Specific

NOTICE. Please be warned that this house in no doubt filled with toxic gas. Please use breathing apparatus. [27]I (seated at the steering wheel) have arranged this to happen. There has been no murder here tonight. We have all made the decision to carry this out acting completely of our own free will and uncoerced. Please donate our organs to those that need replacements. We have gathered what medical information we can on ourselves. Our bad if it isn't enough; we did the best we could. That, along with contact / next of kin information is on the dining room table, spread out. Also there's reimbursement for downloaded music; will be seen when you check your internet bill.

Also we understand that we only have the place until morning, then a set of tourists get to take over. Please, if possible, be cleared out by then. Soasto not ruin their vacation. Wouldn't want finding us to be their memory of Sam Francisco.

Notice Placed on the Exterior Side of the Front Door of Rebel Lombard's Downtown Residence / Apartment by tenant

---

[27] Color change indicates handwriting change

NOTICE Everything inside is free. Please just take what you can use. Door is completely unlocked. Don't need any of it where I'm going.

Rebel Lombard Letter of Resignation Dated Last Full Day of His Life C / O Manager Hyde

-(date)

I would like to thank you for the good you've done for me. Contrary to my family's expectations of how I would be toward a supervisor, I'm grateful. When I first moved to San Francisco, it was for two reasons. First, it would be just too much for unwanted relatives to endure to come in and harp, among other things. Second, it was an act of rebellion. When I first stepped off the Greyhound I didn't even have enough cash for a big mac. I had to go into a homeless shelter. And whether a blessing or a curse. I was soon in a small sardine can on Golden Gate Avenue a block away from Market Street, which proved to be of convenience, because I was taking BART up to the docks to flip burgers at an In and Out. On a whim, not even sure why. But you were in my backyard and I came in and applied. I was shocked, but you took me in and gave me work as a waiter. I hoped I worked hard and didn't spill too much Pho, seems like about the only non-illegal thing people come into this neighborhood for. On tips I made more than I did ever before in my life (not much, don't get excited). I was truly grateful for to be making more money; and I needed it. You see, I've had a past. And I know everyone has, but mine. Well, it wasn't very good. I needed more money to hire lawyers. And no, I'm not having to defend my-self in court, I'll say that much. Otherwise I do not want to say. But now all legal avenues have been exhausted. That's that. Probably would have helped if I hadn't had a hack lawyer, but that's not on you. It's the straw that broke the camel's back. Any remaining hope, whatever ember there ever was is now out. I should have known as much. What's happened has happened and will no doubt happen again. Life just goes right on, regardless of what is in the path. Thank you for providing employment; I will no longer require it where I am headed. If I may have any say; which I probably can't, I would ask that you give it to someone else that's stuck in this slum for whatever reason. Someone going through what I was.

In other words, I quit.

(signature)

(name written out same as rest of message)

Suicide Note of Rebel Lombard

To whom it may concern or whoever cares. My name is Rebel Lombard, I am in the driver's seat, there is ID in my wallet. I have been the primary designer of this; with assistance from Kat O'Farrell; Yes, I asked her, her parents really named her that. They have all left their own notes, acting in that manner autonomous to me. But I will explain the reasons for my death.

"You can take a this out of the that but you can't take the that out of the this" It's like that. I have memories I just can't forget. I had a bad childhood. I leave this letter only hoping that someone will find it and somehow it will change them, affect them for the better.

I will never forget that party, being arrested and brought home to my parents by the police w/o the slightest attempt to preserve or mitigate. Oh God how exposed I was! I needed to stay with a friend to sleep it off. It was imperative that they not see me like that. In that moment I was a public nuisance; someTHING to just be dragged in off the street and dried out. The gross indignity. And my parents were exactly what both the police wanted and expected. I have since regretted not simply committed suicide by cop that very night. Who knows, maybe then I would have been mourned as if my life had had any actual value.

That night became my life. It was a spiral-scramble. It wasn't the last night like that. I will remember being caught by the side of the road, being in trouble over and over. Got caught with this, got caught with them, on and on. Being in and out of military schools. Eventually it was in and not out. I simply cannot forget their strictness, their severity, their controlling rigidness. And While I know, I know that this is no doubt to you officer a bunch of buzz word claptrap; know this. You weren't there. And I'm trying to describe my own personal hell on earth. But you can't. It just is. Just as the best movie special effects are not the same as the real thing. So it is doubtful that you could really depict it. And even if you could see it; you wouldn't know what it's really like to be there. For to experience that that young an age. With already some degree of trauma and growing in addition! Or perhaps, maybe, just maybe. You do know. You were in such a place. You do know what it's like. Except even then you don't. First of all you had your own experience, you didn't experience the very same, maybe better, maybe worse. But also. No doubt. You gave in. All along I felt them, trying to get into my inner-self. Prying and trying to recreate the true me. Even if they were right. But you. They broke in. I considered just conforming, letting them in. falling into the spiral of just seeing just how much a good boy I could be bending and swaying. I could tell that that's what my parents wanted. A rigged good little boy. Not their true son; no they much preferred a product of expectations. And oh, how they loved that little proper boy inside me they just knew they could cut out of my soul. But you, you are a, a, I'm not sure what. But you're dead. Not like you're just dead on the inside, or some angry "You're Dead To ME!" But you just are dead. You're true self had died (for better or worse) who knows, maybe such that your true soul has actually passed into the afterlife like mine now has. And your earthly vessel is merely inhabited by settings. A form of real-life zombification. Who knows?

As you're probably guessing by this point, yes, eventually I found (was dragged) to a place worse still. A place with a name that should send shivers up your spine. Wherein they merely used whatever crude tools laid at hand to recreate me. (They actually used the word Recreate!)

In the words of Rabbi Kushner *You may say 'I know what you're going through' but you shouldn't. No matter what how close your experience is; you don't know what they're going through. (or at least something like that)*

And so ends the life of an undesirable public nuisance. A former juvenile delinquent just to be spanked and sentenced into obedience and submission; and an up-till-now current minimum wage earner, not worth more than that and with issues and such a personality that the only member of his family that might want to talk to him is; who am I kidding. No doubt they have told her enough even if she could my kid sister would still have nothing to do with me.

Why now? Why not in that camp (not strictly for lack of trying). Rather because what shreds, what scraps of cash I had went toward a search for some shred of justice. But the last ray of hope has been squashed. I could go vigilante; but no matter what there is always some change of it going sideways. Even murder suicide, could go sideways and instead I end up in jail. I can't go back! I just can't go back to that sort of place!! I've been so much authority. I could never describe it; And That's A Good Thing! (Trust my you don't want to truly know what that's like) This is the straw that broke the camel's back.

Thank you for reading what I have to said

(signature)

(name written out same as rest of message)

Suicide Note of Rebel Lombard as mailed to his sister Danielle; Mailed "Return to Sender" Unopened by Parental Units

Dear Miss Danielle G. Lombard,

Hey sis, I'm afraid that this will be the last time you will be hearing from me. Or at least for your sake let us hope that is that way for a long time. Or perhaps this is being read by Mama and Dad; in which case KINDLY GIVE IT OVER. This Is Not For You! But I digress, whatever that means. Let this letter be known at The Suicide Note of Rebel Bart Lombard.

I know you haven't heard from me in a long time; nor do I know if you would want to hear from me if you could (or if you'll ever truly see this). First of all I should thank you for what little you have done for me. Not sarcasm, rather that there was little that you could do for me. But you did. And if fear for what repercussions it may have had on you.

Soon you will be a teenager; and I hope to God that you're teen years are better than mine were. I will not describe what I went through. Partially is that it would be an attempt to describe what cannot be described. But also that I don't want all that over your head. If you can have a good relationship with our parents. Great. Happy for you.

As you know I was sent away many times; with the intension of helping me. It's for the best if you never know what happened when I was away. I hope you can have a social life; a good life. May you get past this. May you not be grounded too much. Be careful, they will no doubt track your phone, put something in the car so that they could track where you go. Harrass your boyfriends, or girlfriends if you happen to go that way (no offense, I've been living in the center San Francisco. And I haven't been able to see you in years).

As for me, I got into some stuff. Admittedly not good. But, the lengths to which they went. Even if they are right. Sometimes I knew they were right, but just how far they had gone. It was hopeless. No chance they could convince me truly by forcing me. But they just kept trying. In time I started standing up for myself. I even had a plan in place to kill them. Mostly pie in the sky; you'll never find it, was only in my head. A few times I physically overpowered Mama. And I guess they got scarred. That's all you need to know. For your sake. Don't ask about it. And you really don't want to talk about it to them. You should know that everything I own I have left to you. But don't get excited. First it has to be in a trust. You're a child so legally you can't really own anything. (Yet I had to be bailed and paid fines; explain that?) Second, I know exactly when the grim reaper arrives, so I'm going to blow it. And last, there was very little to start with, some of which I was giving away.

May God bless you and keep you

(signature)

(name written out same as rest of message)

Suicide Message of Ash O'Farrell as Sent to Her Secret Boyfriend Igneous Belvedere

Igneous, prepare yourself for what you read here. You probably should wait till you have time to freak out. Just trust me

(several blank lines to protect message from accidental viewing removed from this spot to save space)

Igneous. I love you. I still do. But, something has happened last night. Actually this is on some form of time delay so likely more like the night before. I'm sending it in the wee-hours of the morning. We've been keeping things primarily on the down low. But, now things have changed. Possibly the worst fight of my life was then. Too much! I do not even want to begin to describe it. Horrible. They knew everything, or at least a far as I can tell. I'm unplugged and even when and if the day ever came, well. We could never be together. And we're years from any hope of anything like an out-of-state elopement, even if we could get away. I apologize for how I'm notifying you. It's just that I can't really just call you or have a face chat. I know what would happen then and I can't let that scramble spiral. Also if this was a message given in the form of say, a video, maybe an audio recording. I think that that would be even more traumatic. I think.

I am ending my life tonight. It will be painless, I am sure. Please do not bother trying to call 911 or save my life. I have used a time delay, albeit a confusing one. While I do not know exactly when you will receive this. But I assure you that I am dead by the time you get this message.

You have been the love of my life. Please, for me, don't feel guilt. In the words of somebody, "mourn, if you must". But go on. Have a good life. Find the right person for you. Enjoy life. Do good. BE HAPPY. I haven't really died. I've just exited. Furthermore. Have I really passed away? Is there such a thing as having your life pulled out from under you? Is there even such a thing a murder? Or is it just reducing the number of years in someone's life? I have a 400 word limit, so I will simply say: Aloha[28].

---

[28] Translates-hello, goodbye, and I love you

Suicide Note of Kat O'Farrell

To my family and whoever happens to read this. Let it be known that this is the Official Suicide Note of Kat O'Farrell. First to the firemen. Yes, that truly is my name. Second no offence to those that named me that. Third to the police. I have done this purely of my own free will; you can be assured that this was not a murder. Forth to the paramedics. Please act quickly to preserve my organs for donor recipients.

Now for why I've done it. It's been hard the past while. First I left New York City, where I had been born. I had friends, a social life. A great boyfriend. Almost everything a girl could want; sure there could have been more, but nothing worth mentioning here. I was ripped out, inner-personal issues between two different people (well one person and my parents) that sealed it. Not that that wasn't totally on my parents. I had no choice. I was dragged clear across fly over country against my will. I had no say in the matter. I was dropped here, well South San Francisco. And no offense to the locals, I just want to go home. I hold nothing against this city. But, well. Homesick. Not that that's the cause, well, it is and it isn't. Let me explain.

I had had a boyfriend back in the Big Apple, as I have already said. I missed him. We tried so hard, he tried so very hard, to stay together. He really did. Man of my dreams (and before you call SVU, we were the same age). And before you simply call this just another teenage romance. We first crossed paths in 6th grade. It was solid. And furthermore, well. I can't really explain why you shouldn't just belittle a romance by simply chalking it up to a teenage romance. Oh, I truly believe we would have eventually gotten married. Just, couldn't. You know what they say, long distance doesn't work. But no, I didn't kill my-self over him. It was a bit of time that it all eventually came apart. There was nothing I could do. But, while I would want you to do your very best to not let him know soasto not burden him with my death. I would like to say a few words to him; only in the off chance that this horrible message ever did reach him. "I didn't kill myself for you. Not meant to be an insult. I really and truly loved you; still do. Merely, I do not want you to have a burden over your head. All I want for you is for you to find that one special girl, the right one. Have a good life. Decades from now I'm sure we can all meet up and laugh about this"

But what did cause my death? I will now elaborate. You see, I had no life set up here in The City when I arrived. And by in large, it remained that way. I had siblings, and we were held together, like surface tension, by our collusions. (Forgive the big words please). They helped to sustain me. But I was able to bring almost half of my social life with me. It was in cyber-space. I had a life on the internet. That I was able to bring with me. And the joke's on my parents; if you're going to be left with only an E-life, this is the city in which to do it. I enjoyed my life. But, things began to unravel. In an age where everyone it saying "unplug" it would be nice to have at least one person going against. They thought that they could simply unplug me, and send me off to have a social life. But if you unplug a TV, it doesn't make the radio come on. It merely unplugs the TV. I was left with nothing. Absolutely nothing! I imagine you're a typical person looking down your nose at teens, with our petty play romances, and our rude Phubbing. I am sure you can't make sense of any of this. But, just because you can't understand it, that necessarily makes it bogus? Sometimes we disagree with things so much that when we hear something that absolutely flies in the face if everything we believe; we can't even understand the words the other person is saying. Not that you aren't willing or try not to; rather being literally physically unable, sometimes almost as though the other person was literally speaking a different language. Sometimes, some things, some extremes. Either you comprehend it or you don't. There's either no more a way to explain, or there is no explanation. It just is.

For some time I had a lifeline, like air holes in a box. In the extremely unlikely chance of survival I won't give any further explanation beyond that I will be eternally grateful. But in time, it all came crashing down.   And with it; everything else.

Ask not for whom the bell tolls, it tolls for me,

(signature)

(name typed out same as rest of message)

P.S.[29] I understand that typed suicide notes are suspicious; as such I will also stamp out my fingerprints. In the hope of easing any suspicion.

(all ten finger's prints stamped here, at once.)

Suicide Note of Kam O'Farrell

Dear Mom and Dad,

Hello, I know it is a shocker to hear form me like this. No doubt this letter has been given to you by a police officer. I would not have told you these events if but that it might make a change in how things would happen. In English: Maybe this can be a list of your mistakes, so you won't do likewise to Mary.

First of all, this event, it was my idea. Others, who shall remain nameless, planned it. But it was me who first brought it up.

Next, I know I've been reduced. I have simply had pills thrown at me. They make me easier to deal with. They put a lid on me; they make me plyable. Agreeable. And I can't explain it any better than that. I really wish I could, but I'm not Hemmingway. I wish you could have put up some form of a fight when the school district wanted it. But you didn't.

To what can I compare my life? It's like this time when I was little; still using pull-ups. To tell you how long ago. You just kept trying to get me to "Just take a deep breath!" on and on deep breath, deep breath It made me madder and madder. Long forgotten what the fight was over. You couldn't stop till I calmed down and would no doubt also be more agreeable. Even said you were about ready to call an ambulance if that vein didn't go down in my neck. Maybe if you had just left alone. Moot now; maybe. Just kept making me madder and madder, which aggravated you more and more. And you just kept going at it harder and harder. Two different things, each one, couldn't go down till the other did, and just kept at it more and more because the other kept going higher and higher because of the first one. Are You Getting This Scramble-Spiral?!

---

[29] Post script

Actually, it's a bit like Crow's having to work hard to just be somebody else. Frankly I think that that's been much worse for him. But he and he alone is keeping his note a secret; for you two only. Anyway, I've tried to be good. To not need tons of accommodations. But frankly; this is it. My ADD / ADHD is already worse than I thought it could ever go. As you know I've long said that if it wasn't for age; I'd worry over my cognitive state. Now I do anyway. I know there's support, I'm just not seeing it. Just like you. Get that? I'll repeat it. I know there's support, I'm just not seeing it. You so much go on about how you're not getting support; or that you're being kicked when you're down. Well same here. And not just me. A lot of us have similar issues. Sometimes they overlap. Often we will have just one of us that's really bad hit by X Y Z. But at least the majority of us are dealing with it. Frankly I think we both have more in common that either of us want to admit. And you might say, that you only say that once or twice a day. We say that you say it every. single. day. Three, four, five times a day. Which brings us to how we all see things from our perspective. We remember things from our perspective. Both of us. I've read on neurology. That is scientific. Both of us; we hear the other saying stuff about my neurological problem. And to the other, it seems perpetual. Like I said; we both have more in common than either of us would like to admit; like in inverse.

Beyond just saying the same over and over; I know not what else I could say. Tell Mary I said hi. See you in the afterlife,

(signature)

(name typed out same as rest of message)

Suicide Note of Crow O'Farrell

Remember that time, was probably weeks back. I had the radio going. You burst in; I had been listening to something vaguely familiar. Wondering where it was going and hoping to remember. Turns out it was something, let's just say that you wouldn't want me to listen to, and honestly I wouldn't have any problems with that; honestly I'd do that voluntarily myself if I knew. But it was just at the moment that you came in, that it also began to become obscene. I was caught in a scramble-spiral. And by that, I mean you flipped before I could get a word in edgewise. Also I was in such a way that I'd have to move some stuff in order to get up. It all fell down around me as I scrambled to get up, to shut it off. And it just made it worse; the harder I tried to escape, the more it fell around me, even you went so far soasto shove me back into my seat. I could never hope to relay the feeling, being shoved down! Exposed! And of something I wasn't really guilty of! Sure I caught a little; I had heard most all of it before. Five more seconds maybe and I would have remembered, gotten up a little slower. You'd never have known!

And while you'll no doubt just call all just making excuses. Know this. I have often felt guilt; seeing how you treat my siblings. That I didn't intervene. Well this time there's nothing I can do about it. Where am I going with this? I'll tell you. You obviously think Kam needs to just learn to move past her Neurological problems. That she can just work around it. I know that you're not simply too lazy to bother accommodations. But you do think Kam is lazy; it's undeniable. As an ethical matter I try hard to avoid body language. I know little of it and actually wish I knew *less*. Because I believe body language to be a way to stick your big fat nose in somewhere it just doesn't belong. It's a way to worm your way into someone else inner sanctum of their mind. It's a complete invasion of privacy that I do what I can to avoid. But nevertheless I can tell that you really just see her as lazy. I wish that I had stood up for her earlier. But now I will stand up for her. Admittedly after the fact and for only one person on one matter. Let me begin. Do you remember that time we went back home to where you and dad used to live? Remember how Kat got mistaken for a Jewish Lesbian? Well actually, more accurately would be a couple of slurs that I am not comfortable repeating. And it certainly didn't help that she hammed it up moving like a man and kept saying "so what if I am?" till he took a swing at her. Sure we all knew Kat kinda goaded the bigot. And you and the sheriff alike called her out on it. But you knew things simply weren't that simple. The situation probably is, oddly enough, best encapsulated by tongue in cheek children's author, Lemony Snicket "People aren't either wicked or noble…they're like chef's salads, with good things and bad things chopped and mixed together in a vinaigrette of confusion and conflict."[30] Slightly out of context; but only slightly. Certainly not someone you would expect to be quoted in a suicide note, but that's as good an

---

[30] A Series of Unfortunate Events Book 11 (The Grim Grotto) Chapter 10 (pg. 223)

explanation as I've heard. And certainly the case for Kam. Sure she could work a little harder. Sure she could no doubt to a bit better. But by in large. She really does, err, I should communicate, did. Kam really did do her best. She did need more accommodations. She's tired. She's about at capacity. You could understand that time down south that things were not all one way or another. Why can't you see things that way more often? Things are never black and white in this world. There are a few shades of dark that are so close to black they might as well be. And there and a few shades of light that are close enough to white that they might as well be. But there are no true black and white in life. Sometimes we encounter some very dark and light shades. But that's it. We virtually never cross that which is so close it might as well be one or the other. Such is the case of my life.

Let's be honest. We have nothing in common. You're more than twice my age. And I think that's where our issues ultimately stem from. We try so hard to get close; and to do things together. Why? What's the point? Sure you're my family. And you're raising me. But ultimately. We're about as different as can be. Sure there are overlaps. But almost all of which are the product of being brought along on what the other wants long enough that I (or use'd two, goes both ways) have come to like it, or even prefer whatever it is. And sure, there are always fluke exceptions, such as Alexander Book Company.

I'm not the terrible kid you think I am. We're just different. How so? I am careful that you don't overhear what I hear on the radio because I don't need your little subtle judgments; often stuff you can't even pick up on. And it's not like I'm listening to the garbage you so see modern music as. So what do I listen to? You may say that what I listen to is garbage; but that's strictly a matter of opinion. Less talent necessary? That you could argue. But how are we simply different. I fear you over hearing the Christian rap I listen to. RELIGIOUS music. I will not further explain who I am deep down. I probably could really explain. But as a defensive mechanism I have come to be secretive as an automatic mechanism. I simply don't have it in me to be that open; even if you were able to understand it.

We both have more in common than either of us would like to admit. We both have things that we say and that the other hears being said incessantly. For starters with all I have trouble reading people, you often go on about how you can't read me. And on both our counts we read things in each other that are abundantly obvious. Clear as a bell. Obvious as could be. And it's bogus! We both have things going on in our lives that the other side is completely oblivious of; and let's be honest. Doubtful could care less. So often you go on about how hard you try to please us. How the whole evening has revolved around us. On and on and on. And I don't even think you hear it! You don't even see the guilt! You just can't! I can't even explain it. So much of this, it just is. You cannot explain an explanation; you cannot explain this. It just is. Meanwhile I feel like I should just be a certain way. Be a certain person. I should just be the kid you really want. And so I just put on an act, try to act a certain way. Sit still. Be good. Act proper. It's not quite to that degree; but its real. All too real. And I feel guilt; like if I just worked hard enough; I'd truly be what you wanted, like I'm the selfish brat that just wants to hold up in his room that I am accused of. Also I will feel guilt over not actually being that kid, on the inside. And eventually I being to feel guilty. Nowhere near guilty enough to lose sleep; but some guilt. Eventually I told you about this. You probably couldn't have reacted worse; certainly you could have had some reaction. And later on after only a small number of times I had ever said it (enough to count on one hand) you claimed how I was going on about it, or something like that. That I will address further later on. I'm sorry sometimes it spills out. After the move, I gave up. I just did. Not exactly on being that adoring son you want, but more, well. That's probably what you've been picking up on, deep down not caring what you think, I guess. For all that you say that you work to please us (not calling it a lie) I've tried to be that good boy. So much so that I've become paranoid. I am secretive automatically. And I sense danger, abuse of power everywhere now. I feel like I need to metaphorically walk a certain way. I think even you have begun to pick up on my paranoia; I know even I can sense it.

I'm tired. Not the kind of tiredness that comes for exercise; or from being up till all hours. But a different form of tiredness, about as easy and difficult to describe. But one that's just as real.

Also about the exact conditions in which I have been found. First of all I hope you have agreed to transplant our organs. We have tried to ensure that paramedics got here in time for organ harvest; and that no one unknowingly walked into a carbon monoxide cloud. As for the late man you will know doubt blame for all our deaths. Don't. His life has been like that of an old asylum patent. Strapped down; absolutely incapable of fighting anything off, like Catr. Tormented and prodded for his own good. Only less concentrated, spread out over years. Don't take retaliation, there's on one to retaliate against. His family, NO, his parents. They proved to want a proper and up-right son bent into proper shape by whatever means c/o a military school, or something even worse. No matter what I've been though, he's been through what I believe will someday be one of the horrors of history. Not one of the greatest; but a horror nonetheless. On second thought, please retaliate.

On the subject of Catr. So often you have rooted and supported police. You have said that it was such a good thing when cops had the mercy to make delinquents, sit them down and give them a talking to. Oh how you live to give a talking to. But what about when it happens to you? You basically had the same happen to you. It was an inverse. You needed to be straightened out. And-and Oh God! Why am I Even writing This! Their's no way you'll ever be able to make heads or tails out of what I'm saying! What's the point? But guess what? I have a secret. You'll never guess. This one; I can tell you never would have supposed. What is it? I'm not going to tell you. It's real. Don't suppose for a minute that I'm' making this up. I'm taking this secret to the grave. Which in my case is super easy. I'm not making it up, I'm just going to make you wonder, make you scratch your head for the rest of your life! Just like I know you really will with this letter.   I'm about to die; I'm entitled to be a little nuts.

All my life I've to some degree been putting on an act. When I was little, small lies I told on a regular basis. Even then I was to some degree putting on an act. I am holding back, not saying all my internal matters; same reason I tried to keep some of the stuff that I have kept a secret, secret from you, hoping to protect you. But that went down in flames. And by in flames, I mean that you reacted about as bad you could have, barring only a few split hairs. So much of my life, everything that I thought could never happen. Would never happen. It already has. Even things that it never even crossed my mind once would go a certain way; they did! Never going to be one of those people priests talks about living with guilt for not being a better person thinking I could work harder, be better. Never going to change my opinions on (different things) and become part of my own perceived stereotype. Never thought I'd ever truly doubt it you loved me; (came to the conclusion that it all boiled down to what your best happened to be). You'd never do this. You would never to that. Never thought I might drop out (Thought that I might eventually do that to get away from all this). Guess that's another thing that's been lifelong. That candidate's so bad, that could never actually happen. You would never really check out putting me in that.

Never thought I'd consider killing myself. Never thought I'd kill myself.

But there's a reason that I had those two different sentences. For some time before this. I have been suicidal. (Ugh, it's creepy just writing this.) But I have been, could never count the times we've been in a fight, and by fight I mean you going at me, either angry concerned, or just angry angry. Either way, I could never count the times I that you've been going at me, and I just wanted to kill myself. But, I held back, for a time. In fact. This isn't even the first reason I've been suicidal. First time, as I believe I have already communicated, it was after the move. First, it was thinking about what Catr must have been going through back home (mine, not yours) and from there it was expanded to many related matters. They really bothered me. I have even had to be careful what I watched on TV, saw on the internet; at times it's given me palpitations. But it was months, maybe year or more before you even began to catch on. However I tried hard to make you to never figure out. That, at that point I realized I'd just assume die. But I wouldn't really do it. Why? Because, despite what you'd think looking at me (unless you've done me up in a proper little way as you often do, and humiliate me while you think I look so good) I do have morals. Even after all this, for quite some time I held back. Honestly, all the stuff (not all bad, not much concerning) that has floated around in my head, I have kept much, if not most, of it secret, for one reason or another, starting with childhood imagination. For all you think. You don't know me that well. You really don't. And even some of the stuff you've proven so grossly unable to come close to comprehending. For all I believe in forgive and forget. It's not like I don't want to forgive you; it's almost like I feel I shouldn't. Maybe it's how you get so ticked at your siblings MOM and then you go on and on about it; not intending to condem. You've taken it so far you once fussed at me for essentially not repeating back judgmental stuff about your little sister. One of the few times that I have defended myself; and once again you greatly saw what I had to say from your perspective. And speaking of defending myself; at one point some time back I was really being bothered by not being able to defend myself. You Just Wouldn't Listen. I think that that has made me really defensive. When I sat you down, you claimed that I could and that you'd listen, but that I'd just want to keep on forever. Actually that was more after the fact. When I sat you down you just gave me a bunch of excuses. Stuff like having a lot of pressure. I can only remember the vibe, and that I was shocked that you of all people just give excuses like that. Or maybe that was just said something in the heat of the moment, or most likely something in between, I cannot remember much of that, it was some time back. And speaking of how time steam-rolling on makes me forget. I know this sort of stuff has been going on for some time. And despite how bad, how hard it was to go through. I'm forgetting it. Just am. That's my other guess as to why I feel as though I just shouldn't forgive and forget.

But, I'm sure all of this, that no doubt has just hit you. It's really bad; as such I will say a couple of good things about youse. First of all you've never said how my room / Wait! My house! My bills I pay! My Room! Thank you for never playing that card. And indeed, you may very well own the house or hold the rent control. But that's where I spend more time than anyone else combined. It's the one part of my living quarters set aside exclusively for me; and might I add, the only spot in the whole world just intended for me. Well ok, you've kept some of your stuff in my closet all my life where I never dig in that deep; and a few bottles on my windowsill where I also never really ever go, but not the point. You can play the card of paying the bills, and make me feel absolutely helplessly dependent. But it's not your living room. It's intended for me to use. Much like our apartment manager back home was the owner (ok working for the owner, not the point), but he wasn't supposed to go in our apartment to use as his break room or whatever else purpose he'd use it for. But he was supposed to come in routinely for repairs and repairs related reasons. Not exactly to that degree, but like that. Ultimately, I may use the common areas, but that's my own personal sanctuary. It's much like how technically everything in my room that I own I actually is legally your property. Another thing I feel I should thank you for is you never said. "No, when you're an adult and you've got your own children, you can do things your way. But for now, We're going to do things my way. Ok?" NO! NOT OK. First of all, it assumes that (putting aside the fact that this is a suicide note) I will live long enough; and would then be later on committing the same thing as you! Second, you're basically a king (or queen in the case of Mom, makes no difference and I don't care) over me and with power that works in a similar way. Even scripture describes how, when a child, thought loved. You've basically a slave. I wouldn't actually say this, but it is true that I in no way choose for you to me my parents. It just happened. Undeniably you should have some authority over me for my own sake (especially as a little kid). But does that automatically give you absolute authority and power over me? And, to repurpose (and rearrange) your words "Don't be a logician." Sure you could point out child abuse law and etc... but basically. Loco parentis.

   As for it all coming to a close. Regrets. Sure there's regrets. Big regrets. Not having tried to have good friends, a social life as a little kid. Should have gotten more into counter culture, and sooner. Small regrets. When I hit 16 and went up to the mall, I set foot in the Disney store. I got to talking briefly with a clerk. I said how I had loved it as a kid. And how it had changed, and so much since I was little. But now I was older. Wish I had said I was 16, as of that day. Once in a lifetime opportunity to say off-the-cuff. Oh well. (that one was a small one, but did take more space to explain). Other regrets. Never went to Chuck E Cheese's once ever. Regrets so small I've sense forgotten. Like you I believe no man can be good enough to right his wrongs (no matter even if he was one of the best humans that ever lived). But maybe I might be able to undo some of my regrets. Practically (though not exclusively) not having stood up for my sisters. But we sibs almost didn't leave notes at all for Your sake. What they, that is their content, would do to you! (I had never planned to if I had gone through with it; same reason) But maybe they might be able to help our baby sister Mary. Maybe you could learn something from them; something that would help her to not go thought the same that we did.

-Crow

Last Will and Testament of Crow O'Farrell as to NOT be read until his death; not legally binding

Let this loose document be known as the Last Will, Testament, and whatever legal hoo haa of Crow O'Farrell.

All my earthly possessions (including those that technically belong to my parents legally) I leave to the "thug street potheads" you detest so much in Golden Gate Park. They're living my worst nightmare. First there has to be some reason that they're there. Which is no doubt a horror enough. Then being on the run, from truancy, no doubt from drug enforcement, from cops just wanting to blindly send them home. Somehow they got here, or their also on the run from their families, or both. I'd rather just end it all than try to endure the elements and survive through that. (case in point) I know what you think of them, what you will think of this. To which I get to say: Tough! I imagine my sisters think likewise about their possessions; full disclosure I haven't actually asked them for fear of leaving them with the thought of what they're going through hanging over their head as they pass their last bit of time on the earth. Also they might say no.

-Crow

Note to Whom it May Concern Found Scribbled on the Back of Next Suicide Note (Author Unknown)

To Whom it may concern:

F.Y.I.[31] A digital copy of all suicide notes can be found on the computer on which they were first typed. (Try the blue laptop left in the top floor bonus room.)

Collective Suicide Note of the O'Farrell Teens; Ash, Kat, Kam, and Crow to Their Infant Sister Mary Upon

---

[31] Presumed-"For Your Information"

the Occasion of Her Achieving Necessary Maturity for the Reading Thereof

This is to Mary for when you decide she'd old enough to know the details. We know that someday you will have to explain all this to her. And that you'll have to determine when it's time to give her this talk as well. Obviously we'd never be there to speak to her for ourselves; so we have made this letter to her.

Dear Mary,

Hello and greetings. It is us. Your big sisters and brother. We don't know how old you are when you read this. Perhaps you've just learned to read; and found it hidden somewhere. Perhaps you just got your driver's license. Maybe you're older and they decided that you were old enough to read it. Perhaps you're younger, but they decided that you were old enough to read it. Maybe Mom and Dad are ill, or even passed on. You and your significant other are cleaning out where they had been living; you were never told. We have no way of knowing who you are like, what you're stage in life is. Or possibly if you were ever able to see this letter at all. How old you are, or anything. At the time of us writing this letter and our deaths, you are but an infant. Only able to eat, sleep, and inflict parental insomnia. No sweat, no bad, that's cool. Just know that we all love you. And we wish the very best for you.

We wish that we could be there, to conspire and subvert Mom and Dad. And while you may doubt, or have been taught doubts of that, due to the cause of our deaths. Know that the reason we left notes at all was in the hope that it could help you. We all hope to God that you have a good life, and a fun childhood. And most of all, a far better teen-hood than we ever had. Albeit little, we have done what we could to help you out. To help you to never have to know, very well, what we went though.

We're sure that you know by this point how we died; unless you found this letter without Mom and Dad knowing. In which case we would simply ask Mom and Dad to be kind and explanatory (explaining) rather than punishing. You can have them read this to get them to believe it. We all killed ourselves; certainly by the time you read (or possibly are read) we are long gone. And certainly the reasons you have been told (or possibly will soon be told) are no doubt told from a perspective. So we will briefly explain why. Not wishing to take up too much time purely talking about ourselves.

Ash

I am Ash, the youngest child and previously the baby of the family. My death story begins back in what is our hometown. Our being the twins and our brother. I was a New York girl, I really was. But, one day. We moved. I don't want to go into the why.

After I arrived in San Francisco, I had lost everything but my siblings (and yeah, my stuff. But that doesn't matter). I ended up in a correctional school. Either you know what that is, or you're better off not knowing. I will simply reassure you to say that I was never incarcerated. While I was there, I met a boy. First connection I made after I got dumped in The City by the Bay. He truly was a native; if not a vestige of a bygone culture. He was the love of my life. His name was Igneous; hopefully you have met him, or will get to meet him. The move from everything I knew and loved was hard enough. But him, we had to keep it on the down low. And if that expression no longer is in use, suffice to say that that means we had to keep it secret. Eventually we sibs' teck was exposed. With it the relationship; we were forcibly ripped apart.

Kat

I had quite the social life back in the Big Apple. But one day. We simply had to move clear across the continent. I had nothing. Everything I was accustomed to; gone. With two exceptions. My very long term boyfriend. He tried to stay in contact. I wouldn't say we were engaged. But I truly believe there was some unspoken understanding between us that we would eventually get married. He was the only one that attempted to remain in contact after the move for any length of time at all to speak of. And a little ways back even he dumped me. We had just been torn apart for too long. I suppose it was bound to happen. Certainly didn't help, but unlike Ash. For me the real reason wasn't being ripped apart, but being cut off again. I had an E-life. It was the one thing I could take with me from my home to San Francisco. And as such it became a bigger deal. I became a bigger deal. A bigger part of my life. But then one night, for all of us it completely exploded and imploded. In my case they thought that they could simply make me have a social life and teach me a lesson. And oh God could the value of that lesson never end! They would do anything to hammer that lesson in. Sacrifice anything of mine. I will never forget that scrammble-spyral. That's that I suppose. They thought they could make me have a social life by taking away what life I did have. But all that they could do was take away what life I did have. One door closing doesn't prove that another will open, admittedly it's likely that it will get you to try to open another door. But one door closing simply proves it's closed.

Kam

I have ADHD, also known as ADD. Suffice it to say I'm extremely scatterbrained. I just can't pay attention. Used to when I was little I couldn't sit still. Not so anymore. I just can't pay attention. I didn't know it could get this bad. I feel like I'm losing my mind! Like I have the dementia! I never thought it could get this bad. But the real reason is that while I have had a little accommodation. It's simply not enough. Sure I have created a few of my own accommodations (I'm quite good at guessing at how to respond to statements I need repeated, but don't dare ask for them to be repeated) And then, the school caught wind, I simply got drugs shoved in me. I won't creep you out by describing that. I feel that I am losing my mind!; and they are just shoving little tricks at me, like, like I can just transcend this!

Crow

For some time I have been having to suppress who I truly am. I am the reason they took that horrible move. No offence if you're a proud San Franciscan. I have had other issues, and I tried to keep them away from being seen. Including and especially by our parents. I've tried to endure, believe me. I really have. But no longer. And I can pretty well tell how I will be relayed to you by-we-both-know-who. It may be seen as satanic, or occult, or who cares. I will admit that there is quite the element of rebellion. But by all rights, it's simply honestly. Bear with me. I may look dark, but we all are dark where it really counts. We're all imperfect. We may be 98-99% good. But that's water compared to ultra-concentrate ink. Basically, we're all evil, incredibly evil, and the reason that sounds crazy is because we also see things from our perspective. We can see good humans and evil humans. Also it is less crazy when you stop to think how there is good and there is evil. And if only faultless is good enough to be good; then how good is good enough to be good? But we can't really see ourselves as evil because we are so evil; sure there are some people (not my call to say who) that are worse, and some that are better, but the difference between humans compared to true goodness is so infinitesimal. I may not seem like the normal mass going Christian. But I am one; thought not typical. Beyond that I will not say too much about who my true inner-self is. That has become an automatic mechanism. However a little more may be illuminated by my suicide note. Hopefully you will be able to read the notes we all have left

We hope you to have a fun childhood. Have joyful teen years. A good life and good times. Hopefully our parents will have learned from their mistakes. Who knows? You were a surprise. Maybe you'll have a little foster brother (or sister); and if that should happen, let this letter be to them as well. We love you, and anticipate getting to meet you. Though hopefully not too soon. Honestly, we don't know what to say. We wish to say so many great things. Worthy of this context and that would stick with you to have meaning. We only hope that by having left suicide notes that they were good enough, and Mom and Dad were able to open their minds enough to understand and comprehend. That they have some impact, that some good will come from them. Who knows? Indisputably you will have troubles in life. You will no doubt have to face the bigotry that is behind the common view of teenagers. Wherein all teen problems are belittled and teens themselves are seen as so unpleasant, and high maintenance. Like the comic strip wherein the spider said he had hundreds of children, all teenagers, asking to be squashed. (it's an issue hard to sum up in a few short words.) Hopefully you will (like us) be raised Catholic. But also not sent off to school in a demeaning-atomotonic school uniform till you are accustomed and have just conformed into the mental shape that is demanded. We hope to God you have not been sent off to an absolute horror; the man that dies here with us was one such person. But no matter what comes down the pike. Know that God will be there right by you. And if by some chance it is possible; which admittedly we doubt. We will also be right by you. Pulling whatever strings we can for you from beyond the beyond.

(signature of Ash O'Farrell)

(name typed out same as rest of message)

(signature of Kat O'Farrell)

(name typed out same as rest of message)

(signature of Kam O'Farrell)

(name typed out same as rest of message)

(signature of Crow O'Farrell)

(name typed out same as rest of message)

Press Release for in the Event of Any Media Coverage Whatsoever to Speak of

This is a press release for whatever news media happens to cover this. Usually most suicides are not important enough to get into the news. But we imagine that this will be big enough to be an exception. First of all as we have said this truly was suicide; uncoerced, though there are obviously reasons behind this. The reason that this was not sent into KQED, Ch. ** News[32], the San Francisco Chronicle or posted on the internet is simple. While we did want to be found in short order; we did want to Not be found until we were dead. It is for the same reason that we sent a delayed message to 911. We sincerely hope the police can stop being terrified of the possibility of a compromised investigation and can release this letter to the media and public quickly.

Naturally we all presume that there will be questions as to why? Well, in interviews, you'll mostly hear it from a perspective. With ALL of us we have very few people in our lives that know us well and have been in much of any recent contact. We all have been cut off from those we hold dear, know us well, and / or understand us; one very recently. All others some time back that we were severed from them. We will explain on a person by person basis the reasons as to why. And in the interest of retaining interest it will remain short.

Ash O'Farrell

Because of my age I will no doubt get the most attention. I was a New York girl. But a forced move happened. My social life didn't follow me here. Skilling details, in my forced vacuum a native boy fell in. We eventually were totally exposed and ripped apart like a sheet of paper. That's why

Kat O'Farrell

After the forced move I lost my social life in the physical world. The vacuum was filled with my digital social life. I had some time back had had an extreme breakup. But I got unplugged.

---

[32] Television News station requested to be redacted.

Now I have nothing. In this age where everyone says "unplug"; it'd be nice to have at least someone pushing back. I'm all alone. That's why

Kam O'Farrell

I had HDHD / ADD. It was bad. I wasn't running around. Rather it was just the inattentive. First I had these little tricks crammed down my throat. Sure they were probably doing their best. But they were just trying to just make me work hard enough to just transcend it! That's the best description I can really give. And after long enough the school ordered me to be drugged into submission; or at the very least so they wouldn't have to lift a finger to deal with the ADHD. It's not to say that there was not accommodations; but, well, I guess that they were just afraid of babying me. That's why

Crow O'Farrell

I am a complicated and suppressed person. I had lots of internal problems and two parents. I am neither willing to open up enough or to take the time to explain or defend my inner-self. Suffice it to say that I looked one way and was another; beyond perpetually putting on a brave exterior day in and day out. There is also a little more to it; but not much. That's why

Rebel Lombard

I was a tad stereotypical back in the day. From one military school to the next. ANYTHING For Order! What can I say? Eventually, then there was that one last place. I just can't get past it. When any last shred of being able to deny that justice would never happen. That was when I decided that was that; the end. I also fear how much of them was forced in; how much they forcibly changed me. Manipulated my deepest self. Like to send a shout out to my sister Danielle, and my, as of the evening before I made the decision, kind employer -[33]. That is why

---

[33] Did not want to capitalize off what happened. Suffice to say it was a Vietnamese restaurant / Pho House.

We hope that someone can get something out of this story. It's our nightmare. Most of us would have run away if there had been any hope of any real living or survival. Be careful what you hear, in the event that this becomes a major news story, that is, worthy of investigative journalism. We may be baking pies up in the sky, but if this news story ever becomes enough to make a real difference in the world, Amber Alert was started because of just one case. Please, don't let this be used to push for government to claim parental rights. Why? Because look at what parental rights the government already has. Foremost there is the foster care system, which we firmly believe will go down in history as one of the horrors of history. Don't believe us; look at all the countless horror stories, the children that have been wrongfully taken away and the abused children that didn't! And once in, far more stories of abuse, over capacity, and look at the homeless youth in Golden Gate Park. Ask them. Surely there you could easily find numerous who have left for a reason. $10 they'll tell you. Doesn't stop there, look at the schools, they're a mess. We'll steer clear of anything political, but know for all that there is campaigns (albeit often annoying) against bullying, why doesn't the schools simply stop bullying? Other parts often don't make sense such as how you're punished by being expressly forbidden to come to school. Now smart kids (rarely trouble) might take that as a real punishment. But the troublemakers. That won't be punishment to them until their pushing 30 and flat broke. In the meantime their doing things that would land them in prison if they did to a principal of police officer. (assaults, swirlies, theft, etc...) Please, we're not going to actually believe that this is going to make that much difference; especially because the difference it would most likely make we are expressly forbidding (ok so we can't actually forbid it). But we can point out that it would most assuredly be a re-manifestation of already existing issues, no matter how it would work, should government ever claim parental rights for itself. In fact even we don't know what should be done.

Another thing you must keep in mind is that, we will be thought of as a tragedy, something should have been done, in place, blah blah blah. But what of those that didn't? Most likely never even had it cross their mind. What of their suffering? Furthermore it's not simply a matter of some went through something harder than did others, or even an issue of it having been harder on some than it would have been for others. It's undisputed fact that there is pain tolerance. With physical pain two people could experience the same amount of pain and one be virtually unaffected. While the other in bordering on agony. Who is to say that the rule of thumb ends exclusively with physical pain?[34]

Hopefully this will make a difference; and a difference for the better. Hope springs eternal. This (whatever this is) it doesn't take it's origins with us. For example; heed the words of Thornton Wilder-

Uncle Pio never exactly beat her, but he resorted to a sarcasm that had terrors of its own[35]

Collective Notice to Local 911 / First Responders by Means of Text Message (From only Ash O'Farrell, Kat O'Farrell, Kam O'Farrell, Crow O'Farrell, and Rebel Lombard)

(This message has been lost. It was intended to be set on a time delay delivery. A mistake was made. While it remains a mystery exactly what mistake was made or what exactly the contents of the message were; it is safe to assume we have a general idea.)

Suicide Message of Igneous Belvedere as E-mailed From His Electronic Mail Account to His Sister Echo

Hey Echo. I've got bad news. I was at school earlier today; got the worst message of my life. Ash had a falling out with her parents. Apparently it looks like all her siblings did. I got her suicide text on my phone. But you know how our school is. I just handed in my phone and sat down and shut up. I can't believe what's actually happened. After I got out of school by that point there was no hope of saving her. I went up to where it actually happened. They left the door open waiting for first responders. I fast knew something was wrong. I heard the car running. I found her. She wasn't the only one there. I glanced through a bunch of suicide

---

[34] Likely also a lot of the issue with alleged snowflakes
[35] The Bridge of San Luis Rey

notes looking for answers. I didn't take the time to read any of them through, but I got answers. After all that I've been going through, she was the one person (besides you) that stood by me. She was there for me through authority and hell on earth and even her father. And I couldn't be there for her. She's gone now. I went to close her eyes, I rubbed up against one of her sisters (also dead) (couldn't even tell which one) And the feeling. You'd think a dead person would simply be a noodle, with no muscular action going on whatsoever. She had completely stiffened up! I imagine this is a lot like what hell must be like.

All my life, I've been the greatest phonograph repairman in an age of vinyl. I have fit into, if not been a poster child for, a culture that exists as only a vestige. I have been through trauma, I can't bear it. I don't even want to think about it. But no more. This is it. I've decided to stay behind here. I've sat down against a wall. I can already feel myself drifting off..

Transcript of Suicide Video of Echo Belvedere Posted Posthumously by Paramedic –

(sports car running fills background noise; garage is background.)

Echo - Hello cyberspace. My name is Echo Belvedere. I would like to tell something to my family and to whoever else cares. Earlier today my brother died. That's him slumped up against that wall there.

(phone briefly turns toward dead body, back to speaker)

He died after his girlfriend in turn took her own life. In fact all her older siblings died, their bodies are here too.

(Camera turns to show Ferrari full of dead bodies, one door is open.)

They all have chosen to end it all. As do I. Different reasons for each person, but none completely unrelated. Some I knew better than others, the adult driver, assuming he can be called the driver simply because he is at the steering wheel, him I do not know.

(Speaker shuts open car door with her hip; shakes her head)

I don't know enough to explain the details of their deaths, and the notes just seem so brief, so abbreviated, shortened. Compared to troubles that could actually lead to this. A little explanation from me, could never do-

(speaker begins pacing)

- it justice. Justice, something they'll never see. I will say a few words. First of all, my brother lived a hard life. I can and will pinpoint the exact day things went off the rails. But first. I myself used to be that girl with the flowers in her hair. Putting flowers in her brother's hair. I was a stereotypical little girl; I'm not quite sure if that's a confession or a reminisce. Also because of background, I was very spiritual. Always talking about auras and related. I was the very definition of innocence. I still remember clearly the very day my life fell from harmony into crazyland. My parents fell into a dammed form of youthful rebellion against that which was admittedly a youthful rebellion itself. I remember finding my parents watching this show, it was called 'Beyond Scared Straight'

(speaker shakes her head momentarily)

I may know little of the controversy that another of their favorite shows got caught up in, on the same network. But I know that if there ever was an A & E show that should have gotten such an uproar; it was that one. We've all head the words 'I just can't look' I wonder if that is at all any less fiction that is how humans outside of certain positions use only 10% of their brains. At the very least. I have no mechanism. It felt like hours, but someone I trust later indicated a matter of minutes. That was all it took of that show. The illusion, the fairy-word wherein I had lived all my life. It went poof like blowing on a very dusty book. Never again did I ever even want to watch My Little Pony or Care Bears, or anything else. And it didn't even stop with the screen. My parents, honestly believed that it was truly in the best interest of the victims. They thought that they truly needed to be straightened out. That it was truly good for them and they simply were being made into those they should be. I could never hope to convey the true feel, the air, of that moment. Through it all they laughed; till I actually vomited. Probably was the first time I ever actually did that since I ascended up to solid food. Thankfully they were kept busy with the cleanup. I ran to by brother. He was much younger, and remains so to this day. I'm sure I was absolutely hysterical. He tried to comfort me as best he could; I tried to keep him protected. I tried to allow him to remain up there in foe-topia as long as I could. It was very brief. I fear I just dragged him down with me Oh!

(she looks up briefly and begins crying)

I just dragged by brother down with me. Well my parents stupid 'growing up' didn't end with that show. Thing began to happen, to change. They took on a new mindset. That show became my life.

(pacing ends)

You know, it's, it's, well, for all people say they can't bear any more. Or they could never bear this or that. When it happens, it just happens. Barring actually passing out. You can't bear it, but it happens anyway. I guess the greatest horrors of history and our reality, they work that way. There's no chorus of screams of agony from dammed souls. No ghostly-foggy cemetery breeze whispering terrible things in between tombstones. It simply happens. As my friend Crow, also killed in this accursed -[36], would say 'sometimes, even you don't get it when it happens to you until after the fact. Possibly not till time has passed. Looking in like in a window shopper, maybe not.' I don't know what he's gone through, and he doesn't know what I've gone through. I do know that Crow has not been living for some time. Just existing; waiting. Waiting for the day to end. Waiting for the argument to end. Waiting for another chance to do something enjoyable. Growing up he told me he was binge watching long before it was cool. Told me that that was about all the enjoyment he can remember form having been a kid. In his suicide note he described having to constantly put on a façade, or something like that. I tried to hang out with him more, and that serves as one of my many regrets. Oh, I wanted to be more than friends with him. I may be a bit of an enigma, but I think we both were and would have been a good match. But the mention just made him nervous and awkward. Another regret is what I have lived through to see, that I did nothing. I just stayed seated and didn't even need to

---

[36] Word could not be understood

be told to sit down and shut up. Course the few, and mostly more introductory times I did stand up. That got me in deeper. My brother and I tried to be there for each other. Nevertheless, somehow. He seemed to maintain his deepest truest self, hey we're San Franciscans. Maybe that's why it seemed to be harder still on him through it all. Or maybe it's the formentioned window shopper's rule. Course it's worth noting I have long wondered if there was something else on top of everything else. Something I've never been aware of going on.

Me, I feel like this. There's this scene. Imagine a large industrial scene. It's a back alley behind a cyberpunk dystopia. There's lots of industrial stuff, some junk, lots of loose metal barrels. Plenty of sedentary pipes, access routes, alleys, and hiding places. Homeless teens life there. Rarely bothered, but sometimes. However if they ever choose they could be gotten cleaned out in a matter of minutes. It's a real fear, like where to find their next meal, or if their clothes completely disintegrate to rags. Yet, somehow. They do have more freedom than those living inside, under the slave drivers. They're completely exposed. Surveillance to prevent any remotely viable resistance. But, nevertheless. I live there. I am inside how a Hot Topic store looks, I am, I-

(At this point she stops talking, a moment later stuff is momentarily moving too fast to decipher. You hear two thuds. Her hitting the concrete, and the smartphone doing likewise. The video continues recording for several hours, just the unmoving ceiling and the sound of the engine. After hours the recording ends when the smartphone battery dies.)

Content of Officer Quintara's Quote

They get to know criminals by being half criminals themselves, be being of the same rotten world, be belonging to it and then betraying it, by setting a thief to catch a thief and proving that there is no honour among thieves

Chapter Nine

Igneous and Echo

"Oh, guess you don't have drugs after all. You can pull your pants up now," said the officer.

Igneous was just glad it was finally over. He suppressed a comeback and just kept quiet.

"*Well of course*" thought Igneous.

They say it can't possibly get any worse. Igneous disproved that. It was still so vividly remembered that horrible day that his life suddenly swerved off into a nightmare. Igneous thought about that day often.

It was just another typical school day. Both he and his sibling were both much younger at the time. Like was normally the case he and his sister didn't want to get up. Well their mother had heard a trick. If they won't get up and get ready. Just send them off to school in their pajamas. And boy did it work. It was the most readily available method. And it was surly the most effective. And that's all that she cared about. Never mind all that it would put them through. It was horrific. The bullying. For all that they went through. They quickly found that this was going to be something that truly could be a label for them for years. For all Igneous held to being a pacifist, which he successfully remained till the day he died. He still didn't take it lying down. And what he did ran him into big trouble. He became more aware and began to have his bubble of origin absolutely dissolve. Worst trouble he got into however was when he stood up to those being bullied by the faculty. That is; he stood up to the faculty. All these things passed through Igneous' mind, he often rehearsed through them. Not in words, but rather that form of thinking that exists, can only exist, in your mind. Too intangible for words. Such is how most of his girlfriend's sibling's troubles went. He wondered why he had not been able to make contact with them. Not just Ash, he called every number he knew but their house phone. No responses. Till now.

Igneous normally didn't bring his phone to school. Way too good a risk of confiscation. But he was worried. No responses? At all. They talked every day. Sometimes multiple times a day. Though then only brief increments. This wasn't like her. Suddenly his phone went off. It was set to not go off if it was someone like a relative of his. He knew it must have been relating to that. He knew that they hadn't heard it, it was concealed and muffled. In addition to set to vibrate. He had planned to go into the restroom to check it in private. In the off chance that it did happen to go off. Deep down he wasn't expecting it. He checked his phone without thinking. Normally he was so careful; he spent the whole day just keeping his head down. Simply trying to not draw attention to himself.

And what he found shocked him. He quickly started reading it in a panicked sort of reading. Just desperately trying to get information on an emergency basis. He missed most of the message; but he got just enough to realize what it was.

"Ahem!" instructed a merchant of dystopia.

At first Igneous waved him off. He was in a panic; he was still in that momentary long panic-read. In fact he though so little of the man that he waved him off so slightly the man (fortunately) missed it altogether. However that comment, within the recesses of his mind, was enough to (unfortunately) distract him from catching one very important part.

"No Cellular Devices On School Grounds!" the imposing authority was even more clear in his voice that time.

"*You're using you're phone. In fact- Gross! I don't want to see that. Is he younger tha-*"

Then it hit Igneous like a freight train. He fast found himself in a scramble spiral. Like a drowning man in a whirlpool. Only instead it wasn't him but rather someone else that was the one who would drown to death. His personal horrors became both non-existent and indescribable. All this occurred in but a few brief seconds. He froze and panicked deep down. The enforcer was either blissfully unaware or couldn't have cared less about their being anything more than a little thug breaking a school law and forfeiting his phone. Igneous didn't know what do to. He knew he had to save her. To call 911. But they'd never believe him. He knew he'd never really get a full sentence out. Like so often they would say NO BUTS or something tantamount. They wouldn't (or in some cases possibly couldn't) win over the content of what was being said; so instead like his parents. They too would simply attack the "but" in and of itself. Everything was absolutely one way or the other; utter black and white. And even if by some chance it did get out; and someone the words themselves; both nearly impossibly; all he could do was get himself in more trouble. Like a pilot in a crashing plane. He gave up and quickly stopped even trying to get it to not crash. He just complied and slowly handed his phone in.

"Now move along now, wouldn't want to be late," said man said.

"*Seriously? It's not enough to take my phone, also can't have me take too much of your time*?!" thought Igneous

And so Igneous went off to his school day. In the past, mostly initially, he had stood up for others. But now he just tried to pass though. To just get things over with till he has another moment of joy. And when it did come to pass, then things felt right[37]. Whether the school day went by in a moment, or possibly a century, or maybe both. That will never be known. But he passed though it without further incident.

Later near home after just having gotten off the bus at the end of the day:

Igneous got off the bus. One more school day down. He had long forgotten what it was like to go ride down, sit, and receive knowledge. Ok, so he had been forced to be there. And there, at the time he had hated it. As well as all the obnoxious and corny stuff his now late great grandparents had taught him about learning. Normally he would just simply breathe a sigh of relief. Often he liked to walk around. Pretend that his little universe truly was in harmony. Most days he'd even drop in for a visit with his grandparents. Was easy as they lived in the same block. But this was anything but an ordinary school day. He gave a passing thought to trying to look up long lost friends. He didn't know why. He tried to pretend that things weren't so bad. But now. Things just became different. Right when it had happened he would try to pretend that it wasn't that bad. And it worked.

Igneous thought "*I mean, maybe she was found in time, probably was. And tomorrow, I mean is it really that bad? I mean, Well, they, they. It's not like they're going to- Well, there was*

---

[37] "Aim to live your life so that you don't look back, at the end of your life or after some great catastrophe and think 'How happy I was then, if only I'd realized it' – Gretchen Rubin

this one time-" Igneous stopped himself. He remembered something he Really wanted to forget. He simply tried to not think about that. Long there had been something of a mercy mechanism at play. It wasn't that he went through school in shock every single day. But it was something. It was the same something that had allowed him to completely disconnect from his reality today. But now. Would it be back in time for the 7 o'clock bus in the morning? Reality had washed in like a cold, wet, slap.

Ash was dead.

Igneous had failed to save Ash.

Every day he was being carted off to a dystopiaette with no end in sight.

His parents were something that, while they would often work so that they could be together and enjoy each other's company. They were now just something to be endured.

Surely Ash's siblings (closest he had to friends) would hate and shun him.

18 was a long while off; but when it eventually came he would be grossly unequipped and uneducated.

He was alone.

He could imagine her parents. He was that boy they never approved of. She went off and did it anyway. If she had been old enough; would have been an elopement. He would have married her. But now he was just some delinquent, older than her-

"*But not by much*"

That, and now she were dead. Who knows? Maybe they'd go vigilante. Oh! What did Igneous care if they did go hunting the streets with him. Maybe they would go and stab him to death. Maybe not just her parents. Maybe his friends. Maybe Crow would be there. Echo's, whatever they were.

Igneous shook all these thoughts out of his head. Maybe he was in shock after all.

(insert mule picture here)
Houston•Barrow•San Francisco

Igneous looked out at Haight Ashbury. This was their city. This was their part of town. He hit the walk signal at the famed intersection. Here he was. In the middle of the epicenter of their neighborhood, their city. And the only tie die visible was outside some ice cream parlor. He had been told how other pockets of their culture did exist. But Woodstock was the only one he had even been to. Despite all the back to nature; Igneous didn't really like to leave the city. And his parents no longer had any interest in going to another city. HE was a vestige.

"Maybe we'll be gathered up someday, endure long enough to one day have a home for us be built. Who knows? Was millennia for the Jews"

The light changed. Igneous didn't go home. Instead he continued north toward the park. He had taken this path many times before. Mostly just to get a change to go take in some music, or possibly a nature walk. His enigma of a sister had even been known to come along. But this time. He just passed through the park.

Sometimes Igneous wondered how much he really knew. Had he really grown up in that world? He was born decades after the peak of it. The Free Shop had been gone for decades before he was ever born.

"The Free Shop is gone" A phrase that his parents had long come to say. It was now a family saying; no doubt to be last words of itself. Usually Igneous would at least pass through the park but, "What's the point". He turned down the street gap in the pan handle; beginning the long walk up to the fat cat neighborhood. Up, really symbolized a lot.

Night had fallen by the time he got there. The trip itself would have been only about a mile and a half. But those wrong turns did help to lengthen it. In fact the last 4 four blocks he had walked he actually went south! Course it's worth noting that it wasn't exactly early afternoon when he set out. His feet hurt. Oh! What did Igneous care about his feet? He looked up. He wanted to see the stars. But, this was the big city. It wasn't like that trip out to the Arizona desert his grandparents had taken their grandkids on. He thought about that. All the garbage, all the authority, responsibility and a few other buzz words. That stayed behind. His universe (and seemingly his sister's; though she certainly didn't have the same excited interest that he had had) for once had achieved harmony. An eye in the storm of his life. He would like to have taken Ash on a trip like that, he didn't think she had ever seen the cosmos. Oh! The thought of it all just made him want to cry. Why! He didn't let himself get angry. He was opposed to anger, and hypocrisy. Why, so what if he was? His girlfriend had just ended her life, and it's San Francisco; furthermore, oh. Why argue. And with what? Igneous just sat down and cried. He cried for some time; he had already lost track of time and had forgotten to keep an eye out for parents driving around looking for their lost puppy. He glanced; happened to see something on the door. At first he thought it to be a circular; and dismissed it just as quickly. But, he took a better look. Wait. That doesn't look like a circular. He went up to the door; fearing he might simply have been crying outside someone's curb for no good reason. And in a moment; it was worse than even he could have imagined. He rushed; hoping to find somewhere a key was hidden. He even looked in the off chance that a sprinkler was really a key hider. Didn't find anything. He then calmed down just enough he heard the car. He panicked more. A scramble-spiral. He tried to think of a way to break in. Oh! With his past; if anything would get him into trouble; it would be breaking into a house in moneybearu; but he didn't care; he wasn't even thinking anymore. He happened to find that the door wasn't even locked. He rushed in. He braced himself for a blast of smoke; loud engine noise. Pandemonium and chaos as though the house was on fire. Then once again, reality hit him. He hadn't though through his expectation. It felt no different than normal. Sure he had never been in a house in this neighborhood. But, no matter. There was no smoke; couldn't really even smell much of anything. All there was a sound of a car running close by; and a carbon monoxide detector or two blaring away. He ignored them. He rushed into the garage; not really thinking that he could save her; not really sure why. He ignored the fact that the garage was clean to the point of futuristic. He saw she was not alone. He pulled at a car door. Unlocked. Then he realized who some of the other people were. First moment, he had simply thought that it must have been something arranged by the hemlock society. Then, he recognized her siblings. Her sisters, her brother. Couldn't find the baby. Also couldn't recognize the driver; wondered if that was her father. He had only met him once. He wondered if his mother was somewhere else in the house. Seemed that the deadly exhaust wasn't just in the garage. It had managed to fill the whole house. Good thing it wasn't a townhouse or townhome for the gases to seep into the neighbors. He didn't want to know if the mother had died along with the rest of the family. Maybe stayed back to take care of the baby. Either way. Igneous didn't want to see another corpse. He knew he was in shock; though he didn't know just to what extreme. He looked around. Maybe they left a note. Might explain a bit more.

"*Maybe it wasn't all my fault*" he wondered.

The panic mode was still on so he simply rushed through them when he found the suicide notes; he didn't actually sit down and read them. Rather he just rushed through them. But he learned enough. Igneous then stopped. He still was in there with the deadly gas. It was beginning to have its effect on him. He thought of calling a crisis hotline.

"*Wait, nope, took my phone. Great*"

He then looked at the landline, nope. That would be too traceable. No doubt they would simply have a cop come stop it. No, he still hadn't decided, but he knew if he did do this; he would have to be found after the fact. And he couldn't call someone for help if he couldn't trust they wouldn't go behind his back for his own sake. Maybe a payphone? No, he had the change. But surely if he could find one it would take so long, and by that point he would no doubt be found. What if someone overheard? And last but not least. He didn't know of any. He'd have to look it up. No doubt this house no longer uses phone books. Maybe the internet? Something? No. Who knows what you'd find there; and with his luck. Have the ISP routered, or something. And he'd get caught.

Igneous yawned. Then looked at his watch.

Was well into evening time; but not that late. It was already taking its effects on him.

Igneous went back into the garage; to be with his girlfriend.

Strongneck Books

(Insert picture of the Golden Gate Bridge here)

Echo had a fear. There was this cop, he was doing something behind a door, a swinging kitchen door. She didn't know exactly what was happening. But she had a pretty good idea. They were struggling, just struggling and struggling. They cook, something was going to be broken. No, It was flammable. But, he was ordered to, he couldn't. And so the struggle. It really was harmless, but the cop didn't know. You simply couldn't have a police officer subject to Any kind of danger! And they struggled and struggled. THE FRYER! Boom! The cop screamed in agony. The burning oil. Everything drenched! That's what it was!

Another one: a man was swimming. In the ocean, it was at Point Lobos. The police came to arrest him. He was swimming in. There was an undertow-a riptide. He was swimming along the shore to come in, around it. No! Like with her parents, he needed to be heading in, directly in. Unless he was headed straight in, then he wasn't doing what he was supposed to be. Trouble! They were yelling. Firing at him. Bullets? No not bullets. Something to drag him in. He didn't come in when he was told to; therefore he was in trouble. More charges!

Another,

"Mind if I take a quick look around?" said a cop.

"Yes," said the resident.

"Oh, we're just going through, it's just a routine sort of thing."

"I said no."

"Well, if you refuse that shows you must be guilty."

"Go away."

"It'll only be a moment."

(insert mule picture here)
Houston•Barrow•San Francisco

"I said no."

"Are you going against me? Why the not?"

"I do-"

He was going to say "I don't have to answer to you; go away" but the cop interrupted first "Oh yes you do."

"No,"

By this point the cop was just trying to push and shove his way in.

"it's only a mom-"

"No"

"It's just a-"

"NO!" he had raised his voice.

"WAS THAT A THREAT!?!?!?!?!?!?!!?!?!?!" he pulled out his stun gun, and began to threaten with-

ANK!

The E-mail alert went off on Echo's phone.

Echo was glad, she was drenched in sweat, and that had been a terrifying scramble-spiral nightmare; alas the nightmare had just begun.

Normally she had to turn it in for the night so she wouldn't be up using it. But her brother, her school bus always was later. But when she got home and he still hadn't arrived. Everyone wondered where he was. First they called him; but no one picked up. But no one really though anything of it. By dinner the parents phoned the nearby grandparents. Telling them it was late enough they needed for them to send him home, dinner was 5 minutes from served. But when they had never received a visit. Everybody knew something was up. First they went to fetch him from the park. Well Echo and Father that was. Eventually mother decided to go check other likely hot spots throughout the neighborhood. They drove all through Golden Gate Park. Even started looking at other parks. From Mission Delores, to Kimball Playground, to Laurel Hill. Where was he? Parental anger was dissipating, they began to worry. Dinner was left sitting out; they ended up just going through some drive thru lane. She couldn't even remember where. Echo first worried how much trouble he would get in; then kept worrying likewise. She wondered where he was? They began to think? Had he been acting different yesterday. I-I think yes. Her parents came to the conclusion that he had been paying an unusual amount of attention to his phone. Who had he been talking with? What had he been planning? Wha? It-it made no sense. Had he been planning something. Normally Echo would have been as closed minded to her parents as they were. But, maybe? A stopped clock, twice a day. Echo did worry, still primarily about that would happen when they did find him. But? This was crazy. In time she had persuaded her parents to let her stay home, hold down the fort in case he came home. Where was he? It was enough she let her parents know something. Something of itself virtually unheard of. The something was how they often at school would make simple eye contact. Momentary. But today. He had seemed like he was off in another world; with his body just atomotonically passing through. His mind sitting back and simply watching as a passenger in a car passing through something, by all rights not physically present. That's what he had wanted all along; strove for (he was not the only one) Maybe, she hoped he had simply achieved. She had simply tried to keep her head down, not get into trouble. Should she have? Oh well, done deal.

ANK!

Her phone went off again. Now she was home. Alone. Couldn't not take advantage of that. Echo checked her phone.

"*Great Scott it was late, but still, normally I at least Could stay awake to this time. Guess the TV went back to a station from the On dema-*"

Echo began reading the message She was shocked. Could it be real? Despite content, she did call his phone. Surprisingly. It was answered.

"Yo," said a man.

"Igneous!" Echo shouted into the phone. "Oh thank-"

"What Rock? Who are you trying for?" he replied.

"Ig? It that you?" she said.

"What Ig? This is Custodian W-" he replied.

"You're Not Igneous!" she almost shouted

"Lady, Igneous is a form of-" he said.

"It's my Brother's Name! Where IS he! What di-" By this point Echo was shouting.

"No see, I saw it in comfiscation, though I'd play a game of-" he answered.

"You Mean You're One of THEM!" she shouted.

"Well, I guess Yes, I guess I-" he said.

"BURN IN HELL!!!" screamed Echo.

She hung up. It hit her. That was where he was, why no one could find him. She started to cry. Loudly. The kind of crying that in years past would get parental noise complaints. Nowadays. Sure she had pain; but not that kind of pain. She had many issues; but, she never really did cry. Till now. Igneous was all she had left.

She did wonder how he sent the message. Sure it was from his E-mail; that's what got her to open it in the first place. After a little bit of cyber stuff; she found where it was sent from. She almost never snuck out; it was an excellent escape. But whenever she got caught. It was just too risky. But tonight. That's exactly what she did. Which, considering she found that they still were not back yet. It was easier done than said. She grabbed her backpack, counter-confiscated her Justin Beiber poster and put it back up. And stole some money from her parents for bus fare, and if she decided to stop anywhere for any reason. On her way out she threw her school supplies (and a few CD's of her parents that they played way too much and drove her up the wall) in a dumpster. If she had driven her car, she might have gotten there in time, maybe. But her car was rigged so that they would know; they knew wherever she drove. While standing at a bus stop, she heard the trash truck. They weren't getting that stuff back. She had hoped to save her brother. As for emergency services, well, she was too afraid of what she would be throwing him into. Deep down, she had a pretty good idea that it was already too late. Probably used a time delay. She didn't have exact change, so she walked a few blocks and bought a 1 day passport. She didn't know how exactly to get there, or if she would have enough money to bribe all the drivers to make change (or one might not take a bribe). The bus proved to be really slow. She had pretended to be normal at the corner shop, but by the time she presented it, she was a mess. She tried to keep to herself, but she (in varying degrees) cried all the way to Pacific Heights. She had only ridden the bus a few times before; only alone without permission. Mostly she rode the bus for fear of being found walking along the sidewalk. She tired what she could to keep from being visible when waiting for a transfer. Once she ended up missing the bus. She preemptively blocked any number that could be her parents. They tried to get through but were blocked. Eventually, and on foot for the very last part.

She arrived. Echo first found the place because the front door was left open. Not completely open, but certainly not pushed to. She jaywalked across and got closer, when the road noise ended for a moment she heard the sound of a car idling.

"*Well if that isn't suspicious; guess this must be the place*" Echo thought.

She walked up to the door. Then she happened to notice a truck she thought looked like her parents. She jumped inside. Not about to risk finding out for sure. She could not be caught here.

"*Have they been out all night?! Oh, probably wasn't really them,*" Echo thought, rubbing a belt buckle scar on her back. She closed the door shut behind her. She started to lock it, but the main lock required a key from the inside; furthermore. Who was there to be kept out?

"Oof!" Echo tripped on something, unexpected. She looked around. She found a switch and turned on the light. She found what tripped her.

"A piece of pap-" Echo said out loud. She picked it up, and as she began to read it. She dropped it. It was worse than she had imagined. Her main hope had been that a double suicide (Igneous and Ash) was just so unlikely. Anything more still, in the middle of this crisis. She dismissed just as quickly. But the part she had skipped over...

Echo picked it back up. Ash didn't just die; her whole family was dead. Except her parents; and didn't they have a little baby? Now she was really alone.

"SHUT! UP!!!" she screamed at the carbon monoxide detectors; not really thinking; just nebulas, free floating emotion. She rushed to find her brother. She turned on every light she could find. In a couple rooms she could see he wasn't there before she found the switch.

"*Oh, Why did they have to turn out all the lights!? Who's going to be getting a night's sleep*?!" thought Echo.

Finally, she went where the deadly gas was (she thought only the garage was a death chamber) Instantly, she was shocked. Not by a powerful amount of exhaust, or an overpowering stench of death. But, she was surprised at the smell of death at all.

"*If it takes a while for us to be found*, this smell will be what gets us found," said Echo.

Quickly, she could tell everyone. There was Crow, and all his sisters in the back, and the driver, must've been Rebel. Didn't know him. She started to reach in, turn the car off, then, she found him. She had expected to find him somewhere in the house. Maybe with his head in the oven, probably wouldn't be good enough with knots to be found hanging. Certainly couldn't take the pain of a knife. When she didn't find him inside; she had simply assumed he did it in the backyard. To be near what nature there was to be had there. Seeing him there shocked her. He definitely hadn't been dead as long as the rest. She walked over to him. There he was, slumped over, sitting against a wall. Same clothes he had been wearing at school. Maybe, no, no, maybe, maybe there's still a chance of saving him

Chapter 10

A man approached his car outside a restaurant. He suddenly stopped; it had lojack so they wouldn't steal it. But it had been stripped. He had been here on lunch.

"Figures, guess it was just too expensive," he said pulling out his phone.

Later:

A police car pulled up, the officer got out. Clearly, the man's face said "What took you so long?"

"So, you called in saying you're car had been vandalized, or robbed, err, something?" said the officer.

"No, it spontaneously turned into the popemobile, wadaya think?" he replied.

"Meh, good point," she said turning her head and seeing it.

 "I'm sorry, my bad. Please don't arrest me for that," said the man.

That got her irritated "What kind of dirty cop do you take me for? Crime is the #2 overall cause of stress. At least it is for me that is."

"My bad, it's, it's, well, this hasn't even been my first encounter with law enforcement in the past fe-" he said.

"Last time they simply made off with the whole thing?" she asked in a sarcastic, humor-attempt sort of way.

"Uhh, no, not, not exactly. In fact not at all," he said.

"Got arrested for something? Join the club," she said.

"No, nothing like that! If only I merely had been arrested," he said.

"Sir, could I see your driver's license," she said thinking there might be a warrant out for his arrest, and seeing him wince, she thought that that was why. Not realizing it was at the "sir."

After a pause, he said, "Yeah, you can see the insurance too if they haven't stolen it officer."

She mistook him for asking her name "Quintara."

"Oh," he replied.

She really doubted he had a warrant out for his arrest. Sure he was acting that way (as far as she knew) but, why would he have called the police if that had been the case? As such she went back to her squad car to run it through.

"My bad," she said returning, "Thought you might be wanted for soemthin,"

"Yeah, no. My last encounter was, how we say, stranger, no that isn't quite the word," he said.

"Any of my business sir?" she asked, "And yes, I would like to take you up on that insurance thing if you got it."

"Just chillax, please. Had enough authority for-" he said.

"You too?" said the officer.

That little nothing, off-the-cuff, comment took him by surprise, "Oh! And for the record I thought you'd want to get it yourself for some, police, forensics, reason."

"Whatever," she said, "And for the record I hate to be the bearer of corrupt and incompetent news, but I'll hand this case off. And it will be promptly tossed in a black hole of police reports never to never be seen again," she said.

(insert mule picture here)
Houston•Barrow•San Francisco

"Yeah, I know," he said.

"Yuck!" she said / shouted in surprise.

"What?" he said, "They put something in the glove box?"

"No, sorry. Just a lot of dirty Kleenexes," she said.

"My bad, bachelor pad on wheels, literally. Haven't always even been bothering to take out that trash when I gas up," he said.

"Yeah, well don't feel bad. I once found a to go container from Burger King in my squad car," she said.

"What's so terrible about that?" he said.

"I hadn't eaten there in I don't even know how long. I'm on a diet," she said.

"Yeah, I had been on one myself," he said.

She realized then two things 1. The insurance papers had blended into the snot rags on the floor. 2. Something serious had happened.

"I-I found the filt- I mean insurance," she said.

"Was wondering if I had been going around without it," he said.

"Sorry about what happened," she said sympathetically.

"How do you know what happened?" he said.

"Oh, I don't. All I know is it was severe. None of my business I'm sure," she said genuinely not trying to pry.

"Meh, no doubt already heard about it," he said.

She turned her head sideways.

"Aaa, doesn't matter, err, isn't relevant to this," he said.

"You sure. Say its murder linked and they'll impound it, comb it for evidence, and probably still not solve it," he said.

"You admit to that?" he said.

"Probably won't come back to me. Often I'll make little comments to strangers I know won't come back to me," she said beginning to run the thing through the machine.

"Like that little comment about authority?" he said.

She did a pause, and by pause, that thing where people freeze up for just a moment from what they're doing, with the intension of resuming. After a moment, she said "Relatives, leave it at that."

"I'm sorry, didn't know," he said.

She did it again and said "Neither did he."

"Sounds like the case I just walked into," he said.

"What do you mean?" she said surprised, stepping out of the police car.

Before she could say something about not prying (as in like none of my business) he said "You heard of that mass teen suicide?"

She dropped the thing she was holding, clearly she was shocked. She mentally scrambled; not sure how to handle herself in front of him. She really didn't want to have to figure out how to conduct herself with the father, err, a father in this situation.

He made a guess, and guessed correctly. "No, no. I wasn't one of the people responsible."

She was surprised; but by the fact he worded it like that, figured it had to be true.

(Long pause)

"Then, who are you then?" she asked.

"I'm the guy that found them," he said.

Her jaw dropped again.

After a moment she said "Well, should have known. Figured a responder wouldn't have been that shaken up."

"You'd think," he said.

"I wasn't terribly shocked when I looked into it. At first I thought that it was a murder, I mean, all at once, and being siblings?" she said.

"Forensics debunked that quickly," he said.

"Yeah, I first heard about it on the scanners," she said.

"Oh," he said.

"Yeah, work with one of the guys they sent to the O'Farrell's school." she said.

"I imagine they brought in counselors after that," he said.

"Not just that. A story like that. That's explosive. They actually had to rush to be the ones to let them know. Much like how they had to inform the families. Simply gathered them all up in the auditorium. Told them all at once," she said.

"Were you there, when they broke the news?" he asked.

"Oh no! they know not to let me near a school. Though sure am glad the Belvedere's school is getting them; needed counselors since day one," she said.

"You saw that place, they realized you would protect the students, or is it more of a jurisdiction thing?" he said.

"Officially, jurisdiction. But yeah, basically," she said.

Then the light began to dawn, "You were sent-"

"Yeah, try to straighten me out, so they send me off where they know there's more bad students, yeah that sounds logical. Made me who I am today," she said.

"And that thing about your dad?" he asked.

A fear flashed across her eyes. He realized how he shouldn't have asked that, but before he could apologize-

"I HATE HIM. Oh how he tried to straighten me out. ALWAYS saying how he was going to put his foot down. And It was always true. He always would and could find a way, he always did just put his foot down. Harder and Harder," she screamed, talking 90 miles an hours. "LIFT YOUR FOOT UP DADDY!!! DON'T PUT YOUR FOOT DOWN AGAIN!!! IT'S TOO FAR ALREADY. LIFT YOUR FOOT UP. DON'T GO MORE. LIFT YOUR FOOT UP. LIFT YOUR FOOT UP." By this point she was on the ground. Crying.

"Oh, my God," he said.

"I've never said any of this to anyone," she said.

"I don't understand. Why are you still subordinate to him? You're a grown woman. You're a-" he stopped himself.

"You can say it. Pushing 40. Probably won't ever have kids but hey. I was eventually able to move out, even was able to move up here," she said.

"My God-" he said.

"He controlled me, put out bells and traps to keep me inside. At times I worried that he has put GPS in me. Thank God that it was before the days he could make me carry a cellphone to ping. He always watched me like a hawk. It was predetermined that I would be a good girl and my purity would be maintained the he would have to meet any boy I wanted before-hand. Shortly after I left home I came out-" she said.

(insert mule picture here)
Houston•Barrow•San Francisco

"Oh-" he said.

"It was bogus. But, kept him from harassing me about finding a nice guy. Clearly he had been struggling to accept me; needless to say he's been floundering. But, I've learned how to act, so he doesn't question it. All the time I lived there, after 18 even. He controlled me. Checked up on me, everything I did. And I don't just mean going out for the evening. I loved sneaking out; it was such an escape. But, when I got caught. It was just such a risk. And as you can imagine; by one way or another. Got into what was, shall we say, not the most savory crowd. And oh, my life was just such a scramble-spiral" By this point she had grabbed some of his dirty Kleenex, and blew her whole face. "Sure, I know he was right about some things. Though I'd never admit it. But, at some point, you've just gone too far. Even when I know he's right. It's hopeless. You've just gotten my mind so closed. So locked up tight. A tight little mind. Ironically he talked about not being too open minded; something about being recruited as a prostitute, or satanic sacrifice, or something absurd. Also I found this boy. Being down in LA, naturally he was a gang leader. He reacted about as you'd expect. When I hit 16. We were going to run off. I talked to this guy at our church. The preacher. I told him everything. At least about running off. It was the strictest of confidence. I will never forget when he said that he'd agreed to keep me in confidence. But for my sake, he went to my father, he used my name. Some claptrap about it needing to be done. I wish I had passed out. I prayed for shock paralysis; never happened. He never got a clue. So many things, each one. Things he said that for most people would single handedly have ended it. It began to feel closing in on daily at one point. Though it was probably more like every 1-2 weeks. Or more infrequent. After that, was a good long while before I ever saw him again. For a few years, I'd seem him. Never more than once a month. I pretty much knew he had other stuff going on; but I was such a schlub, I shrugged it off. Before I moved off. He died. Was just another gang death, and treated as such-"

"You think he did it?" he said.

"When I was LAPD, was able to breach the case file. Didn't look quite like a standard gang kill. Timing was sure suspicious," she said, "Every 6 months I find a pay phone and tell them it was him, anonymously. Never say why. Never use the same one twice. Past few times that's been getting hard."

"You think that'll keep it open?" he asked, "I figure you, a cop, would know."

"This is a cold case gang hit, and reasonable chance that he's actually innocent. Only way they'll solve it is if he goes into a psychic / medium and confides in Benedict Arnold," she said, "I'm so sorry. Not your fault. You know, for all the relief I expected. All this I've never told anyone. And, my mother had a friend. He said how when you tell a secret, it loses its power over you. Pah! Never been so for me. All I've experienced it how when I can't keep it a secret, then and only then can issues arise. Whether it's a parent that doesn't know how to mind their business or internal conflict and issues. If you can keep it secret, no problem," she said.

"But now you're free," he said.

She laughed, and cried at the same time. "Oh no! I would like to have just checked into a homeless shelter on my 18th birthday. But no. He had my brother. And that part about never telling anyone, mostly true. However lawyers. They have confidentiality. I looked into suing for custody. And I'd probably loose. If I did, even then still there would be time before I got him. I can't leave my brother defenseless like that. I watched out for him. Tried to keep things as safe as I could for him. And as things would have it, before I moved out, mother died. She wasn't, well, she never had any problems with him. But after that. He married a much younger woman. Why any woman would want to be married to my father. Besides that he's my father, I'll never know. But as murphy's law would have it. Just as my brother was gaining his independence, they had a baby. My brother had issues, but nothing like I had. But then I realized I'd have to dedicate my life the same to watching out for him. Years down the line they had another boy. Between you and me; I think boys were all my father really ever wanted. They don't know all that happened. And like Ms. de Montemayor from an old Thornton Wilder novella, he realized that he couldn't control his daughter from across an ocean. Or in this case 100s of miles. Kind of appropriate. Me and him can't get along; and neither can our cities," she said.

"Guess that means you hope LA falls into the ocean more than anyone else in this city," he said.

"There's doubt?" she said.

"Good point," he said.

"As for the part about mostly true, well the attorneys. They I told most of it. I think they had a pretty good idea there was more, but they didn't pry. Honestly I do not think they were very good at their job. As a cop, I've had to go in for psychiatric evaluations. But obviously I didn't tell them this. To sustain plausibility I told how me and my father didn't get along real well. Ever sense that day, could never tell someone when I can't trust that they could maintain confidentiality," she said.

"I've begun seeing a professional. And she said how they can't relay information unless they have reason to believe you're a danger to yourself or others-" he said.

"Oh I am. I've been waiting for the time to be right. For it to be safe to just go end it all," she said patting her served handgun.

He didn't know what to do.

"You sure- I-I mean. Maybe. Just don't them that- It, it could be better. Maybe once they're grown you could fly in his face," he said.

"When I was a teenager. I wanted to run away. Made a couple of attempts. Realized wasn't safe. He'd hunt me down and bring me back. When I was past collage age, still hadn't been able to move out. Then I decided I wanted to end it. But I couldn't leave my brother the face his wrath. In time I was able to get to attend the police academy. In recent years, even transfer up here. He very slowly lost power. Once I was on my own I was sneaking out all the time. Up here I can basically do whatever without fear of him finding. But I do have to put in a lot of work, trying to please him. I mean, Many years ago; when I was barely a teenager; or maybe a tweenager, don't remember. I tried, I really did. Eventually I ended up giving up. As for now. I still have to work a lot harder than you'd think. I know he's still capable of what he did. If things ever went back; I know I'd go ahead and do it. Now, well, my life had just been waiting. Waiting to sneak out, waiting to do this, waiting to not be subject to that. Now, I can sneak off almost unlimited. And do whatever. But, what's there to do? Oddly enough that's why I became a cop." she said.

"You don't think being free, would,-" he said.

She shook her head, "No, been trying for some time. Not much left of me. Just here on the planet to look out for my brothers, and just for kicks. I think there's another on the way! No, If I thought out profession help, well. He's been trying to change me. Get inside me. I have felt him being absorbed. I know I've been changed, not willingly. I fell like, within myself. I've just been holding on, holding on for dear life. Barely at all. If they 'fix' me. What will be left? What will happen if I were to let go?" shook her head again. "No, in fact that's why I became a cop. I saw things. I know things. Couldn't hope to describe. I've considered letting 'it' or 'them' or whathaveyou in. Figured someone would be wearing this badge. Might as well be someone less evil. Then, as a cop. I saw things. What was going on. And, I fear I have become what I hate the most. I've seen, well, I saw it from behind a badge; and on occasion bullet-proof glass. But I knew what it really was doing; that is as much as anyone ever could. I've hoped and tried that I was doing some good. A good word in juvenile court. On occasion not running as fast as I could. But, If I were to go all the way. Would I just flush it? They know I'm not one of them. I wear a badge because I have to; but I hate that badge. Maybe I'm making excuses, maybe."

"You're right in the Go Set A Watchman[38] paradox," he said.

"I don't follow," she said.

"It was Harper Lee's[39] sequel to *To Kill a Mocking Bird*. The paradox of the book was the Atticus finch, he said, basically, how he had to compromise with racists, otherwise he would just be too far out, tossed out. Basically not be able to do anything for-" he said.

---

[38] Harper Lee
[39] Tol-ja

"When I heard that it was a first draft, and published by taking advantage of an old woman with dementia, I decided I didn't want to support that and didn't buy it," she said.

"Well, you were left to wonder, was it true? Or was he a racist? Or possibly it wasn't true; but he honestly believed it was," he said, "At least that was my take when I read it."

"You know, that really does help. Guess I'll have to check that one out of the library," she said.

He lent a hand to help her up.

"So, you really don't, umm," he said.

"I find fun stuff here and there to do. Kill time, go out and do something fun. But basically-" she said.

"Your life is ruined," he said.

"I never got over him," she said, "But, though it all. Well. Often, when things are good. It's hard to tell they're good. Best way often is too look back at how badly the bad had been. Does that make sense?" she said.

"Yeah," he said.

"Well, my point is. Through it all. I could never go back. I could never. If, by some method. That, well. That would be that. I wouldn't hang around. I've gotten room to breathe, and,-" she said.

"You'd be gone," he said.

"Yeah, I'd be gone," she said, "Especially, with modern technology."

"What do you mean?" he said.

"I, I see it now. It existed somewhat to some degree when I was a teen. They know nothing about technology. Maybe you'll even get in a fight caused by how clueless they are. Maybe not. Perhaps you try to take advantage. They fall for it like the fools that they are. And, and. When it didn't work. It. It spiraled! I-I I was exposed. He knew what was going on. It was busting out the seems. I tried to keep it from him. I tried so hard. I was powerless. Utterly exposed. It all ripped off to show off my humiliation. I-I couldn't stop it! He saw me as just some bratty little liar; trying to deceive him! And I-I-"

He didn't know what to do. He couldn't just slap a cop, even if she was hysterical. Could he?

"Quintara! Quintara!" he said. Actually, more shouted. If that hadn't worked; he would have grabbed her by the shoulders.

By this point. It all. She was completely hysterical. Her walls, for this one instance, had come crumbling down. And her with it.

"I don't think I'm fit to go back to work," she said still sobbing.

"I don't think you are either. Is there anything I can do? Is there anyone I can call?"

"Call, Pah!!" she said, expecting a para-hysterical laugh, then after it didn't come, she said "Call someone. Who's there to call? I have virtually no friends. None I would want to see me like this because of this. And the only family I have, that I have any use for is my brothers and their families. But, they don't know the 1/10 of it. And hopefully never will. You're the only one I can trust; and you. Only reason I even know your name is because I had to see your ID to prepare the report for your insurance," she said.

"Oh yeah, Forgot about that. Well, as Maserati would indicate. I have a lot of money. Don't need the insurance. I'll just pick up a cheap Cadillac at the first dealership I pass. As for this. Let's just wait for them to tow it," he said.

"Did you just say cheap Cadillac?" she said, "What, Like a beater or lemon?"

"Oh yeah, like I said. A lot of money," he said.

"Well, whatever," she said. Still upset and shaken up.

"You sure you don't need to call your station, or something?" he said.

"What, and let them know how I've imploded on the job. No way," she said.

"If you ever want help relating to anything with your father-" he said.

"Pah! There's a lost cause. He's a closed mind. Safe and sound, locked up in a tight little mind," she said.

"Ouch," he said.

"Yeah, I've seen that spirit all over the place. We think things should be a certain way; and if they're not then they have to be punished and that you can just enforce things hard enough. Have steep enough penalties, you can maintain order and etiquette and just enforce things by means of fear and intimidation. And any resistance; well. You get a snitch. I've seen it so many times and in so many places. And while I'm sure this just sounds like anarchist propaganda; know that things will happen. It's bound to happen. We like to point out reformed, whatever, those that have turned to the straight and narrow. But, think of what they've been through-" she said.

"Yeah, sounds just like this kid, well, kid isn't he right word. He was, he was the adult. He was sent away for so much of his teen years. Perpetually towards the end. And, and, for those that tried to break his rebellion, to straighten him out. Life just goes on; and they face no repercussions whatsoever," he said.

"That's the thing about justice. Doesn't undo squat. What's happened has happened, only on the crime shows (and not normally even then) does justice ever in any way undo anything. Undeniably we need peacekeepers, and children cannot just be sent out into the world on their own. Someone needs to, well, we have so many people already. Saying that, going on and on beating the drum that gravity falls down not up. Speaking of Isaac Newton, his laws of motion so greatly affect everything; universally," she chuckled and said "Literally, is it so insane to believe that his 3rd law of motion applies exclusively and solely to motion?[40]" she said, "I mean,

[40] For every action, there is an equal and opposite reaction

you see tectonic plates, then in turn have internal places and sub-faults. And the pattern repeats itself not just in big ice-hunks in your freezers. But also in world religion. Any religion will have different sects. Especially in a major religion. In the Catholic Church there's different orders and such. There's even off-shoots in Scientology. Again in cultures, most any nation will have its own culture. But, different parts of different nations also have their own local cultures. Especially a large country, certainly the case with America. So, it makes some sense to believe that this scientific law would also have a transferability to an otherwise unrelated medium"

"Yeah, he described how those that have given in. He described them as dead; Basically they've given over and are just another part of the opposing machine, and ultimately, deep down, hold no real difference. No, that wasn't it. But, he was thinking in that direction," he said.

"And those that don't. They're just some juvenile delinquent scum, just a threat to public safety, some sneaking out brat. We rarely say it. I would assume they rarely think it-" she said.

"Well, there's two different forms of thought. You see. There's words said aloud, but within your head. And obviously there's the subconscious. But, a third form of though exists, not unconscious. But, it's where we think things that you haven't put into words. It (usually) is too deep to even conjure up an image. Rather it's how we have images that are blurry, without context-" he said.

"Where are you going with this?" she said.

"It's also the knee jerk, It's how your mind it pointed. Words can't describe it; or at least words that could be put together by anyone but a poet only literary elite could understand. It's just too intangible. But, the way your mind is pointed becomes apparent in our initial reactions, the way we do things and believe things should be. Even in our prejudices," he said.

"Yeah, we think things should be a certain way; and when it's completely off the rails insane. Then we, I, there's a look. A look of 'wait-, wait, no? no.' but, unless it's extreme-" she said.

"Not always even then, Echo learned that the hard way-" he said.

"Who?" she said.

"Echo Belvedere?" he said, seeing she wasn't recognizing the name, "One of the victims."

"Yeah, seen that too. Course, there's the issue, once again. Not only how far is too far; but just how insane is insane enough to give off an inadvertent enlightenment?" she said.

"Well, so many things, we see them so different, just if there are displayed, by someone that thinks things are a or b. Often can't even put your finger on what exactly, or even if there is a viewpoint from which they are displayed. But, when you back up. Same thing just displayed differently," he said.

"Yeah, I've heard stories of kids, been through so much. But, when they look from a different perspective. They realize that they have simply returned evil for evil. That their brilliant plan, guide them to the straight and narrow, was a lash back just screaming to stay inside the lines, sit up straight, put out the proper etiquette. And they're have been many cases of kids, I've tried to help kids get help. From a means simply other than a backlash, simply a scramble-spiral to get them to act properly. Rather realizing that they need help. Often, gone so far, they can smell if you're at all pointed in that general direction; and you will be fused with the very thing you wish to fight where it matters most. That is. Their mind," she said.

"You know, that mind thing must be right. First of all, I've read a fair amount of research, while they were a bit more technical. And may have been better at wording. They were saying essentially the same thing. Second, that would explain, while I agree with all you're saying. You're very hard to understand. It's just so hard to word!" he said.

"Yeah, well, guess that explains a lot. Surprised I haven't heard a lot about that-" she said.

"Well, I haven't heard about it much more than 2, 3 times. Stumbled over it more than anything. Say, you want to go grab a cup of Joe?" he said.

"Nah, I-I should probably get back to my shift," she said.

"You so sure you can do that?" he said.

"What? Write a few tickets, grab a donut-" she said.

"What if something happens, something major. And I thought that donuts were just-" he said.

"Oh, that's far less common than we make it out to be. And as for donuts, in defense that started out when cops would be walking their beat at all hours. Donut shops were all that was open," she said.

"You want to run the risk?" he said.

"Well, I-I mean," she said.

"Think, think, you of all people. You're in a position of authority; would you want to be stopped by someone in this shape?" he asked.

She paused up.

"Sorry, if I used guilt, -" he said.

She said "Meh, I'm in a position of authority. I need to be held to a higher standard. But if it's still available. I'd love to take you up on a bite to eat."

"Well, I just ate," he said pointing with his head toward the restaurant.

"Oh, yeah, my bad," she said embarrassed.

"De nada[41]," he said.

"Well, this is about the time I get to go eat," she said.

"It's ok, wana go over to Westfield. You could grab a bite and I'll grab, well, I'm not sure. But I'm sure we could find something," he said.

"Westfield?" she wondered if he was just trying to show off, or was really that rich.

---

[41] Translates-it's nothing

"What, I'm buying. Compared to what happened, anything you could order would be pocket change," he said.

"Yeah, that's gunu be expensive to fix," she said looking over at his car.

"Oh, yeah, forgot about that," he said.

"Yeah, I couldn't care about food less at a time like this," she said, just as her stomach began to rumble loudly, "Well, maybe something. But not expensive. I'd hate to feel like a freeloader."

"Well, you could drag my anywhere," he said.

"Wait" she said as her stomach rumbled again, "Something I'd like to show you before we go."

"What's that?" he asked.

"A quote[42]. It's one that I feel is applicable," she said, walking to her squad car, "It's one of them I circulate. So that it won't become something I just stop seeing," she said.

"That's a good idea," he said.

"Oh, not so sure about that," she said pulling something off the sun visor, "Memorized them been going at it so long."

"Well, that sounds like not such a bad thing," he said.

"Regardless, this one is too long for me to be able to relate accurately," she said showing him.

"Oh, he said.

"Yeah, I've seen that myself. We send people in undercover. Turn people against each other. Leave them caught in a scramble-spiral like drowning men alone together in the ocean. Each one trying to survive. We make people betray each other with a wire. Or make them

---

[42] Dr. Hyde, Detective, and the White Pillars Murder.

testify against each other," she said, "Which is not to say that that is necessarily wrong. But when we toss people into an artificial whirlpool of deliberate confusion and lies. Pit them against each other, tear them apart so we can make another arrest. And leave me all alone," she said.

"Say what now?" he said looking up.

"Yeah, Juvenile. Issued a restraining order. Said to stay away from my friends. And they exposed everything to daddy," she said.

"With all that was going on?! They left you all alone with no one to turn to?!" he said, "Was the court blind-"

"Yes," she said, "And I already had no one to turn to. But; they did make for a nice escape when I was able."

"You ever try to catch up?" he said.

"What? Me. Now. A cop? Please. They burned that bridge. These words were written[43] regarding private detectives. I have no idea if they are true. But I know, that I have seen this. Not to say that it's all that or that that is all graft. But that is what it is. Let's don't lie," she said.

"Divide and conquer?" he said.

"That's just one," she said.

"So, where would you like to go?" he said.

"Somewhere where no one will recognize me," she said.

"Wouldn't want this to get back to your father-" he said.

"Yeah, no kidding. I-I- I mean. I, so many times. I gave in and compromised and said what he wanted. I apologized exactly to his liking because if there was the slightest amount of

---

[43] By G. K. Chesterton

excuse or even explanation. Then it's not really an apology. Though, when I received an apology from him, yeah that did happen. Didn't apply. He'd explain. He wouldn't take responsibility, absolute and complete. And-and that's ok. That's reality. But could we not have the double standard!? And, and, And all the times I gave in! I acted proper and simply submitted to your wishes and demands- And It Wasn't Good Enough! He- HE Wou-" she spiraled.

"You're trying to describe something that cannot be described. There truly is no way to convey just how that feels. To say 'You just had to have been there' is an understatement," he said.

"Yeah, that makes sense," she said, "Certainly could never hope to explain what it was like being ripped from my one true love. For all, trying to get to be together. Our most desperate pleas were just annoying him."

"Who knows? Maybe you'll live to see him dead. Or would that just leave you with-" he started to say "A complete void." But before he could get to it. She had a blank look on her face. So blank. H had never seen anyone with such a blank look ever before. He knew he had sad something he never should have.

"After all I've been through. I-I just can't afford false hope. The let-down. I-I could not-"

"I'm sorry; my bad." he said.

The next day:

"Yo,"

"Sup,"

"Still in your work clothes?" he asked.

"Yeah, big bus went off the East Bay Bridge. Thought they'd need all that they could have," he said.

"Oh no, how bad. Or is there some professional-" he asked.

"Hardly, was empty except for the driver," he said.

"Was he ok-" he asked.

Shook his head.

"Sorry I ended up late; Never been here before. First started to go to the one in the Jewish Museum," he started.

"Oy," replied the paramedic.

"That's the truth of it," he said.

"Hi, welcome to Wise Sons Jewish Delicatessen-" the server started.

"Hey Abi, make it the usual," he replied.

"Ok, shocker there, and for you…" said Abi.

"I'm new here, what's good?" he said.

"Well, I normally enjoy what I'm getting today," he replied.

"Then I'll have what he's having," he said.

"Great, coming right up," he said hurrying off.

"You know, I don't know why. But this is the one I like the most. I come here regularly," he said.

"I could tell, funny. Would have thought that you would have instead preferred the mothership-" he said.

"Oh no, I don't much like that one. I much prefer to come here to the ferry building. Not sure why," he said.

"Me neither- Wait," he said.

"What?" he replied.

"What did I order?" he said realizing.

"Vegetarian Reuben," he replied.

"Oh ok, wait. How does that work?" he asked.

"Trumpet mushroom," he replied.

"Well, I guess that's San Francisco for you," he replied.

Getting off the small talk, the paramedic asked "How are you doing?"

"Oh, checked into Galleria Park Hotel, unannounced. Been staying there till I can find something more permanent," he said, "Probably till one-"

"I once answered a call there. A bit expensive," he said.

"Oh not very expensive. Well, you must remember where I had lived. Course now I'm trying just to get rid of that place," he said.

"About that place? What was the deal with the tourists you said would stay there while you were in Europe?" he asked.

"That was a bit of an exchange, a bit. It was a group of gay businessmen from London-" he said.

"Gay, in San Francisco. That's not a stereotype at all," he said.

"Yeah, well, they planned to stay here for some time. But, well. They had a United[44] moment in New York. Had such a good time stuck there in the big apple. Decided to spend the rest of their vacation there," he said.

---

[44] At the time of this being written United was an airline getting out of hot water for having sent law enforcement to violently attack someone; in order to boot them off the flight. In this context; it means being kicked off a flight.

"Do they know?" he asked.

"Know what?" he answered.

"You know, the obvious?" he asked.

"Why? Saw no reason to tell them. Payment even still went though. Obviously don't care; but," he said.

"Actually, you really don't want to tell them; because by the time they would have arrived, would have ended better," he said.

"What do you mean? They could have walked into-" he said.

"Yeah, not exactly. You see, Lombard was gone, so were the O'Farrells. But not the Belvederes," he said.

Jaw dropped, "You-you're-you're right. That never occurred to me. If someone had gotten there first. There would have been someone to tell the news to Igneous, and he wouldn't have been all alone in a state of shock. Someone to calm him-"

The paramedic replied "Or if that text had worked. Not sure what happened; but, who knows how many lives the organs could have saved."

"You got any clue what went wrong? Not exactly the age group that wouldn't be good with working their phone," he said.

"None, my only guess is that he wasn't used to sending a delayed text. Any other time it would be simply have him hit the button later. Must've made some sort of mistake," he said.

Shook his head and said "Glad it wasn't a townhouse, could have-"

"I don't think that they would have done it in a townhouse," he said.

"Makes sense," he said, "You know, when I lost my job in silicon valley-"

"Oh! So you're one of them that's jacking the rent up for the rest of us," joked the paramedic, "Poor taste?-"

"Meh, well. That's why I flew off to another continent. Wanted to blow off steam. Had been, shall we say; not a good working situation for some time. Eventually I was fired; and on bad terms. Bad enough they simply cleaned out my desk for me. And I thought it was bad when they smashed some coffee mugs boxing them up! (They were probably as mad as me.)," he said.

"So, you still out of a job?" he asked.

"Getting a new job has been the very last thing on my mind. Come to think of it. I'm not even sure that I've thought about it once between walking in and finding them; and now."

"Wow, so, you're staying in a hotel. Not the Ritz Carlton, but not quite sleep inn, looking for a new place to live. No job-"

"Don't worry about my finances. I have a lot of money. Look, that house. It's not even the only one I own. I actually own a bunch of rental properties in and around the bay area. I own 2 in Berkley, 3 in Oakland one each in Sausalito, Tiburon, Larkspur, Vallejo, one on Angel Island, one up in Napa, and best part of a dozen on our part of the bay. I'm all over the place like McDonald's. The rent from all that property alone is enough to keep me ok. Course might have to live way out in Hayward. But, can't complain. Not in the wake of this," he said.

"So, you're doing ok?" he asked.

"I'm sure, admittedly money has been the least thing on my mind. Haven't even been paying attention. I'm fine. Err, well, my finances are fine. I'm fine moneywise."

"Oh, well, that. You-" he said.

"I come from money, not that that makes any difference," he said.

"Refill?" asked Abi.

"Oh, thank you,"

"Yeah," said he.

"What yeah?" he asked.

"I, Don't know," he replied, "Never mind."

"You know what gets me? By that I mean just, what are the odds?" he said.

"What?" he replied.

"Ash and Igneous? Really? Serisouly? I mean in the wake of this tragedy; doubtful that's what anyone's really thinking about; but. Well. You know there would have been jokes if they had been out in the open; but. Well. Guess there won't be any baby pumice," he said.

"Well there's that one," he said.

"Well, there is that; but probally the first, last, and only. Have you ever responded to anything like this before?" he asked.

"Hardly. Not to say that there aren't some cases, that don't haunt me. I'm sure that anyone in this line of work has that," he said.

"Really? Like this?" he said.

"Well, this, this is unprecedented. But, I do have some cases that haunt me. One, I had initially worked in Texas, near the coast," he said.

"Like Corpus Cri-" he said.

"No, not as near as we are here. Was in Houston; where I started out. Still have cases that bother me. One, this poor kid. Dispute with his parents. Tried to just jump out of a moving car. Whether safety minded or simply decided that they needed to put their foot down-" he said.

"Please, don't say that," he said.

Surprised, the he said "Oh, my, my bad."

After a momentary pause, was said "Didn't mean to cut you off."

"Oh! Well, he got dragged. Parents wouldn't let go. Siblings were with him, in that car. At that time. That's something you just can't unsee." he said.

"For all that there is violent media, and we are more accustomed. It's not the same. When you walk in on something. In person, that's real, that's different," he said.

"Yeah, another one haunts me. Little girl climbing a bookcase. I believe it was. A boy tried to pull it off of her. Was certain it took an hour for them to come. Put himself in the hospital just trying." After a pause he said "She didn't make it."

"Wow, wouldn't want your job. Just, have you even known anyone that responded to anything this unprecedented?" he asked.

"Oh, not so unprecedented. Youngest I've ever heard of was an 8 year old boy in Cleveland Ohio. Think it was bullying-" he said.

"8 Years Old! How could that be! That-that simply couldn't have been an actual, deliberate-" he said.

"Just what I thought; all while they were playing the news story. Story was how they were exhuming him; mother decided to bury him with a tablet. Have something to play with. But they were going in, he had died early in the year; mid-year he was being exhumed. Looking for evidence of bullying. One of those times that you'd think they'd put a warning label on the news story itself," he said, "But professionally. Personally. No, I have, well, nothing, it-"

The other guy simply shook his head and said "Thought suicide was just adults, some collage age. Thought teen suicides were very rare, in terms of total statistics. And almost always older teens, bordering on adults. Thought I had heard stuff about tweens having those sorts of issues. But, it seemed, how you say, blurry. And so's my memory."

(insert mule picture here)
Houston•Barrow•San Francisco

"Think that's been flashing through my head, is. How. You wouldn't want your parents to come and live with you. Was hard, like it is for a lot of people, when they had their maternal grandmother come live with them for a while; at least was for the parents. But, that's understandable. For a child to have a parental overseer, after their an adult. Even if they get along. Though naturally if they don't its worse. But, isn't it just logical to assume that that might also overlap to affect teenagers? I mean when they're getting older, beginning to take on adult-" he said.

"You life in a country wherein a 15 year old is completely subordinate to (let's not split hairs here) the power and authority of her or his parents; because a fifteen year old is not mature or old enough to fend for themselves or make decisions for themself. Meanwhile a 13 year old can be incarcerated at an adult correctional facility while awaiting trial as an adult because what they allegedly did was so heinous," he said.

"Yeah, in the foster care system. You can argue about whether or not certain times children are taken away, is corrupt or not. But they take away children, put them into a foster care system that is at least bordering on being synonymous with abuse and generally I believe one of the modern horrors of history in progress right now," said the paramedic.

"It's like, how can the city pounds kill animals by sucking out their lungs? Because they are the same body that manages protection from animal abuse. They aren't about to bring down the heat on each other, certainly not themselves. And then; who else is there?" he said.

"This city, there's been so much. It's one of only a few cities in the world that had been complete destroyed, well Mission and Noe Valley were largely spared. But, we're the only city I've ever heard of that's had a mayoral assassination; and the guy got a slap on the wrist for the most rediculas excuse I've ever heard-" he said.

"Yeah, I've heard that story. How any prosecutor could not defeat something so off the wall; I'll never know," he said.

"Yes, just, earthquakes! Fire! The Zebra Killings, the Zodiac, nearly having the worst civil engineering disaster in history, on the Anniversary!-" he said.

"Titanic sank on its maiden voyage," he said.

"I know, just, when the city was destroyed. At least then the Chinamen were finally able to (albeit ve sa ve lying) bring their families across the pacific. But, what's the good in this? There have been many missing child cases, that, while they were either never found or did not survive. They did lead to new measure for safety, Eton Pates, Amber Alert. What the purpose in this? It-it's just-" he said.

"It's a shock, something so great, so terrible. You just stand, you stammer, you're baffled how, how something so terrible could ever happen?" said the landlord.

"I don't know. I know that they brought out counselors to the punishment school. Something they should have had since day one," he said.

"I thought that schools did have counselors?" he said.

"Well, Punishment school. It's just to punish them, I have responded to calls at such places a time or two. I'm not a politician, the 'students' assuming they can be called that at all. They are not little angels or Anne Frank, believe me. But, the way they are treated. My mother once worked briefly as a school consoler. And they only let her into the portion for the disturbed, or something like that. And even then. It was in what had been an old horror-of-history-turned-pop-culture-type asylum. She, and she's someone that has no problem with stop and frisk, she told me she was told not to come in when they were checking the kids in. That she didn't want to see how they were treated, that it would just distress her. Sure it's not word for word. But, she actually relayed that to me," he said.

"I heard of a school that got in hot water. Made boys (at least I believe it was boys) take their shirts off to get checked for gang tattoos," he said.

"I hope the DA, wherever that was, made it into a sex crime," he replied.

"Press charges! For that! Pah! You've got a better chance of Kathy Griffin[45] being appointed commissioner of the Secret Service," he said.

That got a minor chuckle.

"You know, speaking of all this. I think a met a woman, the other day. Like that-" said the landlord.

"Like, what?" he asked.

"What, no! That like that, no, the, boot camp, punishment, Juvenile-" he stammered.

"Who?" asked the paramedic.

"Ironically, a cop," he said.

"Say what- That sound's-" he said.

"Like the definition of hypocrisy? Yeah, you'd think," he said.

"Just happen to get to talking, or need I worry?" he asked.

"Oh, my car was stripped. Petty matter," said the landlord.

"Oh, you ok?" he asked.

"What? Oh, don't worry about me. Simply found it post-facto[46]" he said.

"So, I take it. You got to talking," he said.

"Oh yeah, and. It was heartbreaking. I saw just how much she had built of defenses. One person betrayed her trust, I believe it was she was about to elope. But, ever since then. And the control. How he watched her. Still she hasn't broken free. Now, told me how the only reason she still exists, to do what she can for her brothers. When the step mom is too old for

---

[45] Famous comedian turned infamous after posing with a realistic faux decapitated head of the President of the United States.
[46] Translates- after the fact

more and the youngest is ok. She'll just grab her service weapon. And leave them," he said, thought is wasn't easy.

The paramedic reacted about as you'd expect. But the landlord said "Look, she's been through so much. What could we do. To lock her up in a funny farm, that would just be cruel. And what else is there? Try to talk her into counseling? I dare not harp. She'd just been through so much. Face it. She's been simply waiting for everything to be settled to do this; more than half her life.

He reacted with more shock at hearing just how long "More, more than, how, how old is-"

"First of all, I didn't exactly ask her age. But she made the decision in her later teens. And has been waiting for things to be ok ever since. How her father prided himself on having saved her from her. Wow, how much restraint she must have had to not simply kill him in his sleep," he said.

"You, you think there's anything we can do for-" he asked.

"No, asked. There's nothing," said the Landlord, "In time, she got room to breathe. Some. But even still. Now, there's a void. She has freedom, but-"

"It's like when a surf got kicked off the manor," he said, "They lost everything. Including their family who would inevitably starve without them, they were 'allowed' to stay on the manor. They were then free. Had nothing but the clothes on their backs (as least I assume they weren't sent of naked) but they were free," said the paramedic.

"Sounds about right. Just, wish there was something we could do," he said.

"Maybe there is," he said.

"Like what?" asked the paramedic.

"Maybe we can tell their story," he said.

"How so? I mean, so far all we've done is one internet video. And even at that. Wasn't even us that made it," he said.

"Yeah, you posted it," said the landlord, "but, that's a start."

"Some start," said the paramedic.

"Sonic the Hedgehog started out an air freshener in a racing game," said the landlord.

"You a gamer?" said the paramedic; at any other context he would have cared enough to be both surprised and skeptical to highly skeptical.

"Something to take my mind off it," said the landlord.

"I've been delving into teen literature myself to take my mind off it," said the paramedic.

"Some here too. I started reading *Miss Peregrine's Home for Peculiar Children*. And believe me, it's a great book it really is. It doesn't base itself off anything pre-existing in literature. It makes up its own mythology! Completely independent and just as original. In a world where everyone strives for originality Ransom Riggs achieved. Course even in that; there was a part wherein some kid / teen got upset / choked up about some sheep having been killed. And at that they just took at as him having done it, and he was shipped off to the mainland for prosecution. That part was hard to go through; other than that-" said the landlord.

"Yeah, I got into the second book. For once, the claims that it's even better than the first were true. Still continuing. Still, excellent. Though even then I can imagine what it was like to write. But, even still there was this scene, they had been captured. Got to the point where they already couldn't fight back, couldn't resist in any why whatsoever. They felt so powerless that eventually they'd rather die than give in. I only plot spoil because I feel that it, how you say-" said the paramedic.

"Like the plight of Rebel, and Quintara," said the landlord.

"Quin-tara?" said the paramedic.

"The officer I mentioned, someone, their story needs to be heard," said the landlord.

"So, I mean, how are we going to tell their story? How do you propose doing that?" said the paramedic.

"I-I don't know," said the landlord

"Maybe a movie could show what happened," said the paramedic.

"What happened, yes. But, first of all, I'm Mr. Bags-Of-Money. I am not Bill Gates. And I have no Hollywood connections," said the landlord.

"Perhaps, but, last time I was in City Lights they had a whole display of books that had had been made into movies. New books, not anything close to classic," said the paramedic.

"So, you want to write a book; hoping it will be made into a movie?" said the landlord.

"Well, umm Well," stammered the paramedic.

"You don't know how to depict it," said the landlord.

"Yeah, I mean, even visually seen. You'll get greater detail; facial expressions, voice tones. Detail you won't get in a book, except maybe with an overthought writing style that won't ever actually sell. Think about it. We have researched. We have put in late hours putting this thing together. But, have we walked a mile in their shoes? Beyond that, do we know how their shoes fit, and fit to them. What it's like to get a blister in their shoes?" said the paramedic.

"Yeah, I mean we know what they went through. But at the same time, we don't know what they went through. We have no idea really what that was like. How exactly they experienced it. What that was like for them specifically. How it felt for them. What it was like to them. How it was in the light of their experiences and world view. We ultimately have no idea what it really was like. Let alone to take it and show it to the world," said the landlord.

"Well, in a book, well. With the greatest and most grotesque horrors. You simply see the gore, the, the whatever. And that's basically it. You might hear from victims. But this, this is more, Well. Obviously this is not one of the greatest horrors of history. I'm just trying to explain how it's so hard to illustrate. It's much harder to pin down. Because it's much harder to see. It's harder to take down-" said the paramedic.

"Oh we're not going to take it down. It's a part of the human experience. It's, well. This came up with the woman yesterday. It's intangible. So intangible-" said the landlord.

"We could tell what events happened, we could show how they reacted. We could show the outward signs of what was going on and how they tried to hide them. We could (at least theoretically) transcribe their thoughts. At least the ones that were in words.-" said the paramedic.

"Yes, in fact exactly, but, it. It is something deeper. It's, what they went through. What that was truly like. It's something intangible. They couldn't put it into words. It's like a though, or possibly a mental picture. You have a general idea. But you can't get it clear. You don't fully understand it yourself. You certainly couldn't explain it. You might be able to lead someone in the right general direction. But that's the most you'd ever be able to do. You yourself are merely being pointed. Nothing that can be displayed in a format we as 3 dimensional being can truly comprehend. Rather the closest you can come is something nebulas, just steps above sub-conscious. Deep in the inner-sanctum of the human mind. Something that continues to elude science. That's where it took place," said the landlord.

The paramedic nodded. "I feel like Ignaz Semmelweis."

"Who?" said the landlord.

"By all rights, he first discovered germs and invented hand washing. Deal was, he was over a ward in a great Vienna hospital. And saved many lives implementing a hand washing policy. The death rate plummeted, but the doctors resented having to wash their hands after performing autopsies, so the policy was ultimately rejected. History has vindicated Dr. Semmelweis. But in his time, he was just an annoyance. Where I come in is that; it is at least believed that knowing what difference it would make if people would simply wash up. But no one would listen to him. He died in a loony bin. I too, I'm haunted. I'm bothered by what is going on," said the paramedic.

"Losing sleep?" said the landlord.

"You're not?" said the paramedic.

"Of course I am, it's just. You're, Forgive me if this comes across insulting. It isn't meant that way. But, you're a paramedic. Surely you must deal with tragedies all the time," said the landlord.

"Oh sure. Just the other day. You know how a water heater, if the pressure release isn't working properly. It can become a pop rocket and go up through your celling. Well, that happened to a house over on the edge of the Richmond, at the end of 35th Ave. Hit a young couple jogging through the park. Killed one and maimed the other. Second most unbelievable thing I've ever seen. Homeless person thought that an asteroid had simply come down. It was clear it was man made; but. Just, wow," said the paramedic.

"Yeah, but I mean. Seeing stuff like that day in and day out. Just, I would think. How could you-" asked the landlord.

"What's sometimes worse; is when I can get to sleep," said the paramedic.

"Nightmares?" said the landlord.

"You too?" said the paramedic.

"Well, not as many as before I made sure my little sib was ok. In the light of all this I had to makes sure was doin' ok. I mean more than just a quick little check. But, I think he'd doing ok," said the landlord, "But I take it, for you it's worse."

"Yeah, it's the same dream. And, it's with a horrible air. The sort of air that only a dream could ever have, a little like the deep conscious we've discussed. There I am; surroundings nebulas, not worth the mention, or at least the fit in, but I never pay attention. And then, along comes these things, being. They're so calm. They have a coating of love affection. Concern and care. They say turn back, they want me to turn back. Earnestly for my own good. They are truly concerned about me. But, back. It's not hell, or at least not exactly. You see, back. It's death, it's destruction. All it is. And I keep expecting for the exterior to dissolve, melt away, occasionally for it to evaporate. It never does. That truly is who they are. They aren't demons or evil spirits, or whatever. They genuinely want what is best; and keep trying to lead me, guide me," he paused if in fear or something else, "Steer me." He shook his head to clear that and then said "And as for what you said about me being a paramedic / first responder. Yeah, well you'd think I'd either not take it personal and handle it robotically. Like how most people hear news stories. 'Fatal accident, oh great. Better take back roads.' But, if I did. This case wouldn't bother me. Or on the other hand. It would all be as if I was a coincidental bystander. But. It's not the case. The firefighters often talk about cases, worst things they've ever dealt with. Cases that 'If I could have one fire have never happened' We had counselors come out to the firehouse after that; make sure we were ok. That was shocking. However, as for what I've seen, what I see when I respond to a call. That, as of recently, hasn't been what's been keeping me up," said the paramedic.

"Afraid of something like this happening again?" said the landlord.

"No, outside of Heaven's Gate and Jonestown and etc…, this is the most I've ever even heard of. No, My real fear is that, what about those that didn't? What about them? Surely others, many others have gone though as bad; even worse. But they didn't take that irreversible step. And no, I'm not demeaning. One of them directly spoke of this," said the paramedic.

"Sounds like the woman I met yesterday. As best I remember it. She spoke of how, maybe they did get to whatever we thought they should be. But, what of in the meantime? Even if we are right. What of what it takes to make them respectful, or upright, or whatever. Is it really worth all they go through? People see teenagers a certain way. There's problems, but then there's just, Teen problems. 'Never mind the break up, she'll be over it in a couple of weeks' 'Oh, he's just having swelling of the attitudinal glands' 'You'll find new friends soon on the peninsula-'" said the landlord.

"But I thought that you said how she didn't get over him?" said the paramedic.

"Yeah exactly," said the landlord.

"What do you purpose that we do?" asked the paramedic.

"We tell their story. I believe that we can do," said the landlord.

"You really think we could?" said the paramedic, "I mean, I never was an author. I've in fact never been able to-"

"Pah, no one could. It's not possible to really truly know what someone else is going through. But, we can try to depict the struggle. To show what's going on," said the landlord.

"You want to be Upton Sinclair?" said the paramedic.

"Well, I don't really expect we could have his success. And technically Upton considered himself to have failed, because it was really about the workers "Aimed for their heart, but got their stomach' or something like that. But, who knows, might be Frank Norris," said the landlord.

"Do you really think that he made a difference with railroads? And we're going after something no doubt harder to take down-" said the paramedic.

"Oh we're not going to take it down. It's a part of the human condition. But, we might be able to make a difference," said the landlord.

"Do you think that we can retain any accuracy? Because trying to transfer a part of the human experience. We won't even be showing it. They have died a death of 1000 cuts; just so many things put together, all added up that tooke them to the grave, and it's also trying to take something intangible, something that cannot be seen, or perceived with any of the 6 human senses-" said the paramedic.

"Six!-" said the landlord.

"Taste, touch, hearing, balance, sight, smell. I've undergone medical training; spin really fast, then stop abruptly and stand or sit still with your eyes closed. You'll see what I mean.

Meanwhile back at the ranch. It's something you can only detect by the outward effects. Even if it was a great Hollywood over-budget performance. Still would be hard to see. And to try to simply it into words-"

"We don't have to write a book-" said the landlord.

"Oh, how else could we tell their story?" said the paramedic.

"It's been in the news, maybe stuff on the internet-" said the landlord.

"Unless you're going to commit a crime and be locked up for life. Then if you do it on the internet. You might as well write it in water," said the paramedic, "Books, even after their out of print. Often, especially with the internet. If it was a big enough deal, probably could still find a used copy," said the paramedic.

"Never say never," said the landlord.

"What do you mean?" said the paramedic.

"Remember how you said, you felt like there was an air over the city. Like a fog, but less tangible. Well, I remember having heard a bunch of literary people, they felt the same way after the main library moved and threw away a lot of irreplaceable antique books-" said the landlord.

"I thought that they simply sold them. Having them disappear off into private collections was bad enough-" said the paramedic.

"Nope, tossed them in the trash. At least that's what I've heard. Also heard supposedly that there were a lot of them that additionally had historical value. Course, one always has to be skeptical of what one hears," said the landlord.

"Yeah, it's just. How much do we really know? How well can words convey, oh, I can't even put this into words! How well could I recount the story of what has already happened?! How can I be honest and not simply put in my own viewpoint. And would we include special, mile marker events like pivotal fights that stuck with them? If so that might not convey accurately what things were like day-to-day. What about things that kept happening on a regular basis?

Can we only touch on them? Because if we don't; then no doubt we must have them over and over. Do we know just how frequent? And if we were to do them over and over like they actually happened. We'd be spinning our wheels. Who would read such a boring book? Who could write such an unpleasant book; so full of fighting? And suppose that we did succeed. The real people that should read it. If they ever did read it. They would no doubt be closed minded. They wouldn't understand, and boy have I ever learned, while that claim is often said. Have I ever learned to understand it in and of itself. They'd just say it was simply written from the teen's perspective. And what of what was going on in the parent's background? But it's important that's written from the teen's back ground, I mean perspective. Because that's the vantage point from which they experienced it-" spiraled the paramedics.

"Not necessarily, the Belvederes, they could understand. They could, and did open their minds-" said the landlord.

"Pah! I'll say it again, Pah! They're no more open minded than the rest. It's just; how they were raised. It's like two ends of a line, no. Well, When everyone is utterly closed minded. Those that merely think like you, or similar. That can sure feel like open mindedness. No, I imagine that they've just been shoved along in that regression that, while not necessarily a bad thing. Is so praised and beloved by the older, more mature, traditional, whatever. Just in this one case. Took them an exception-to-the-rule direction. No, they aren't really any more open minded than anyone else," said the paramedic.

"Each and every one of them, had to individually out run us. We, in order to do some good. We have to simply outrun the slowest one of them," said the landlord.

"A true open mind is very rare. We all see things from our own stupid perspective," said the paramedic, "Say, you once said. What exactly was the songs that they downloaded? You once said, but I forgot."

"At My Best, by MGK[47]. Human by Rag n' Bone Man. And 1-800-273-8255 Logic," said the landlord.

---

[47] Machine Gun Kelly

"Fitting," said the paramedic.

"Worst part for me was going to the O'Farrell's funeral," said the landlord.

"Yeah, I saw when I met them. As a paramedic, I've had to go into memory care facilities. And there, I saw the people, they just walked around. They had clearly gone mad, they were utterly lost. I saw that there too. Disagreed too much. Couldn't make heads or tails. And it hit them over the head so much. They were left simply lost. Course it's worth noting how much perspective and seeing what you expect affects your perceptions and both modifies memory creation and retention / storage," said the paramedic.

"Yeah, well, make sense of it, they may not. But on some level; they know. Something has gotten through," said the landlord.

"What do you mean?" said the paramedic.

"Well, I have always hated the idea of someone not even being able to have their own funeral. But, well. It was like after the Gerber[48] family was wiped out by botulism. I remember seeing the coffins lined up. But, on the end. I could tell which one was Crow's," said the landlord.

"Which one? How?" said the paramedic.

"It had dead flowers on it. Old and likely crunchy. Not sure if that's what he would have wanted. But now, they're trying," said the landlord.

"So, you think Mary may have a better time when-" said the paramedic.

"Oh no! They're beating themselves up, as you would expect them to do. No! They talked about their oblivion, and stuff going on behind their back. Getting around the security protocols, what they were doing on the internet. No, it's sure seems to me like that cop's father. Doesn't realize that it's the wrong way. Like when my mother tried to make a more tender roast by

---

[48] Not sure it's even spelled the same actually; let alone if there's a relation.

cooking it faster. That's not the solution; it's the problem. You're too far already. WAY too far. Go the other way," said the landlord.

"Reminds me of something I heard somewhere some time back. Someone, sing / saying bemoaningly 'How could you win? How could you win?' I believe it had to do with just being utterly crushed. Defeated absolutely and completely," said the paramedic.

"We've come a long way. But, we're not totally out of the woods yet," said the landlord.

"We're thinking decades, maybe even centuries ahead of our time," said the paramedic.

"Well, I don't know about centuries. But yes, I do believe that we are thinking ahead of our time," said the landlord "We've made so much progress toward a modern society. But, with all that has happened, can we not now take care of this lesser event?" said the landlord.

"Well, don't know what you are talking about; but first here's two vegetarian Reubens," said Abi.

"Thanks, and-" said the paramedic.

"Be right back with a refill," said Abi.

"Can you make that two?" said the landlord.

"On it," said Abi.

"For me it was when I had to talk to Catr," said the paramedic.

"So, he had phone privileges in the Juvenile-" said the landlord.

"Oh, I have no idea. He had since been released. But, I could hear it in his voice. He was on the precipice of being broken. They just saw some troublemaker. Getting into trouble and making trouble. And that's all they were capable so seeing. Utterly unloved, no doubt all his life. Just someone that needed to be straightened out; no matter what it took. What it involved putting him through. And when he got into trouble. Justice simply had to be served; the whatever- it-was-who-on-earth-cares he did / committed simply had to be avenged. He sounded so close to having his strong will just broken. Who knows, maybe that's what they wanted," said the paramedic.

"Any idea what we could be doing? Anything at all that could help him?" said the landlord.

"If they try to send him away; I say we subvert. And Anne Frank him. But I don't know how we could even to that," said the paramedic.

"Well, we may soon have help in high places," said the landlord.

"How so?" said the paramedic.

"You know that mayoral candidate, the one that's being called all kinds of crazy. Stein... burg, beck Stein, Stein-stein, Well. Can't remember the name, but it was Stein something. He was there at the funeral. Despite accusations, I honestly don't think it was simply an appeal to win points. And I imagine he will win," said the landlord.

"You think he'd help us?" said the paramedic.

"Oh, I'm sure ," said the landlord.

"You really think that the O'Farrell parents are, how you say, ..." said the paramedic.

"Such a lost cause. Yes. Are they in shock, heartbroken, and all that. Yes. I doubt that they will ever even be ok. Are they beating themselves up about it? Yes. Any but both the very worst and most unloving parent wouldn't. But, if they go on to blame themselves by not having clamped down and clenched and etc, then, then,-" said the landlord.

"God help that little baby," said the paramedic.

"Exactly," said the landlord.

After a short pause; the paramedic asked the landlord "Do you truly believe that we could actually be thinking far ahead of our time. I mean, there was a lady like that in the Bridge of San Lois Rey, and, looking back from when that was set to take place. We could see that. But, is it us that is simply seeing things from our perspective?"

Strongneck Books

The reply came as such: "Well, you can't truly be rational and not doubt that, or wonder that. But, no, no man is a hero in his time. It takes at least decades, usually centuries to be able to look back, from far enough and in a different enough time to be able to tell for sure who truly were the good guys and who were the villains."

(Dear publisher, editor, etc & other,

As you likely have come across in your personal life. When a show [kind doesn't matter] has an episode about suicide; at the very end they usually will have something on screen. Like for a national suicide / crisis hotline. A similar thing exists with episodes relating to domestic abuse. I believe such a thing should also be at the end of my book. Maybe for multiple ones; or if this goes international. Maybe US, Can. And UK, or something like that. I would leave it up to them (the hotline) what to put into my book. Only request I might make is that if there is a separate one for teens, that that number be listed first. Also not necessarily just suicide; maybe a number for C.P.S., or a domestic abuse hotline [your call])

Thank you and God Bless,

The Author

From: Escape From Asylum
By Madeleine Roux

Dear publisher, editor, etc & other,

I would like to include an exert from the above named book. I would like to include the first chapter. The book was referenced in the proceeding work. I have many good things to say about this author and the Asylum series both. I am sure that the intellectual property that will be due including this will we worth our wilde. [or however it goes; first time I've ever used that expression in writing] Admittedly it is possible that it will just be too much; we can decide and possibly negotiate that bride when we cross it.

Thank you and God Bless,

The Author

More Quotes

"There's a certain wisdom to this approach in fiction, as in life. When a child dies, when a spouse dies, one feels the grief that one feels when a child dies or a spouse dies. There's no point in trying to describe it. How much does it hurt to have you arm pulled from the socket? It hurts as much as having

(insert mule picture here)
Houston•Barrow•San Francisco

your arm pulled from the socket. Just as some situations are beyond metaphor, some events are

beyond dramatization " – The Shelf, by Phyllis Rose

" Ideological Horror— A horror that frightens and terrifies not ve sa ve the morbid, grotesque, or
macabre, but rather by means of being plausible, likely, or even non-fiction. Often but not necessarily
conveys an Ideology. See works such as The Jungle (Upton Sinclair), 1984 (George Orwell), and Fail Safe

(Eugene Burdick and Harvey Wheeler) Syn-Cautionary tale, Cautionary Horror "

When a movie comes out on DVD; usually they include the trailers that advertised the movie. Why can't the same apply for a book?

Thou Shalt Not Judge

Muck like how brother Juniper investigated the ultimate cause of the bridge collapse, so a landlord and a paramedic go out investigating a septuple (seven) suicide. Read and see the strong-arm and parental overreach that strangled them to death; literally. A dangerous and thought provoking piece of ideological horror.

Other Works From This Author

(insert mule picture here)
Houston•Barrow•San Francisco

The Internal Affairs Trilogy

My broadest, greatest, most encompassing work. With an overall structure all its own. It's more than just an IA novel. It explores all different forms of abuse of power. Both those that could happen and that already do.

Book of Texts

Your school is guaranteed to ban Book of Texts. Book of Texts is the story of an all-out up-rising against the school system from those under it. Told through the communications of the revolutionaries themselves.

Also with a bonus sneak preview of Thou Shalt Not Judge, The Illegal Rescue Duology (Nureal Steinbeck's Hiding Place), and Fire

The Illegal Rescue Duology

Nureal Steinbeck's Hiding Place

First, a rabbi to be, 1950, pulled of the train by Rolph Wallenberg, has decided to try and "Pay it forward"; But After one volunteer session he finds discovers the now known horrors of the old timey asylums. Now he has a new secret calling, sheltering would be mental patents.

Victoria Strongneck's Home for Juvenile Delinquents

Then, 50 years later, a protectee of Nureal's decides to have the torch passed on to her. This time however, instead of a mere handful, she has more protectees and even her own witness protection program. Read and see as tough love and juvenile justice are turned into a horror story.

The Most Frightening Book Ever Written

A dystopian work. A future where an entire religion has been declared a communicable mental illness. Read and see the both ideological horror and horrors of the attempts to stop as well as treat this pandemic.

Fire

This chemical reaction has always had a place somewhere in the horror genera. But never has it been its own sub-genera of horror; till now. A bone chilling book of terror like nothing else.

A Martian on the Planet Venus

Vast Right Wing Conspiracy. Vast Left Wing Conspiracy. Vast Drumstick Conspiracy. ENOUGH! Enough. As you may have noticed; I have tried hard to keep politics out of my books. But Social Politics? That I will take on.

Enter the world of Heresy, a gay evangelical. Who, while he doesn't date other guys; also can't get along with other Christians. See his struggle for acceptance on both fronts.

Please note that this actually isn't a work of humor. Rather that it is a story of how you can disagree with someone's lifestyle choices and what comes along with it, while still treating them as equal and the same.

From the same source as Strongneck books, comes something lighter

Farce Books

After so many concerns having been raised. It's about time we have some laughs.

Edward Fredrick Unluckyducky's Bad Day (And Sequels)

(insert mule picture here)
Houston•Barrow•San Francisco

Murphy would be proud. It would be incredibly unpleasant. That is if it could be taken seriously.

First written years before the Internal Affairs Trilogy, but fortunately edited afterward. This is sure to give a laugh.

The Unluckyduckys

A spin off of *Edward Fredrick Unluckyducky's Bad Day (And Sequels)*. Years after the dust has settled, the bad luck has ended. But the humor hasn't. Also written well before the Internal Affairs Trilogy, and also edited by the author after the fact.

Margaret Holmes

She's the granddaughter of Sherlock Holmes. A tongue in cheek series of mystery short stories first written before the Internal Affairs Trilogy.

43512994R00109

Made in the USA
San Bernardino, CA
14 July 2019